MW01200030

How to Become a
GARAGE SALE
MILLIONAIRE

Make Money on eBay, Online Marketplaces, Auctions, and Everything in Between

Aaron LaPedis

Cover designed by Mara Giulini-Rayborn.

I would like to dedicate this book to my son, Logan, who inspires me every time I look at him; my wife, Sandee, who gave me the support I needed to write this book; and to my Dad, who passed away. Dad, you are a person who will never be forgotten and will always be dearly missed. To my Mom: your guidance, love, and support through the years have made me the success I am today.

—Aaron LaPedis

Contents

Foreword.. 1

Preface... 3

Chapter 1   Your Garage Sale Millionaire Journey Begins Now! 9

Chapter 2   To Buy or Not to Buy? 19

Chapter 3   Negotiating Like a Pro.. 67

Chapter 4   Fakes, Replicas, and Restorations............................ 90

Chapter 5   Launching Your Own Treasure Hunt........................ 110

Chapter 6   eBay: Virtually Limitless Potential.......................... 160

Chapter 7   How to Assign a Value to Your New Treasures............. 199

Chapter 8   Downsizing, and How to Make Money Doing It............. 224

Chapter 9   Putting on the World's Greatest Garage Sale.......... 233

Conclusion.. 268

About the Author.. 270

Foreword

Preface

Chapter 1

Chapter 2

Chapter 3

Chapter 4

Chapter 5

Chapter 6

Chapter 7

Chapter 8

Conclusion

About the Author

Foreword

With this book, Aaron LaPedis has proven true the old adage, "One man's trash is another man's treasure." Aaron teaches us all about the main ways that exist for generating income from collectibles.

As the author of a bestselling book, international business consultant, and cash flow expert, I have always taught in the world of business that marketing is one of the most fundamental things at which you must become proficient. That still holds true, but now I want to clearly make the point that there is another way to make millions! It's simply known as *hunting*. Hunting for great deals or hidden treasures and even unknown fortunes out there, waiting in someone's garage or storage facility; just waiting to be discovered by YOU!

How can you find them? Where are they? What do they look like? How can you plug into this cash-generating business? What do you need to do to locate these buried treasures, these valuable finds that can make you tens, even hundreds or thousands of dollars?

The answers are contained here in this easy, informative, and fun-to-read book. Aaron shows you how to locate, identify, and acquire treasures that can make you huge profits! He also tells you what NOT to buy so you don't waste your money on common junk. This unique book is a fabulous resource and will assist you in your quest to make a lot of money.

Read it NOW and become a real-life hunter of treasure!

Jack M. Zufelt
Author of the bestselling book,
The DNA of Success

Preface

I Am a Garage Sale Millionaire!

That has a rather nice ring to it, wouldn't you say? Actually, there are many Garage Sale Millionaires out in the marketplace. You'll find them at garage sales, in secondhand stores, and attending auctions. As you read these very words, many collectors and treasure hunters, just like you, are looking for and finding the next amazing deal that will make them a tidy profit.

Whether this will be your full-time job or a side hustle, you, too, can become a successful Garage Sale Millionaire. All it takes is a little effort and some collecting know-how; in no time at all you'll be on your way. It really isn't as difficult as you might think. With this book, I will show you the ways to succeed as a savvy collector.

So, what exactly is a Garage Sale Millionaire? A Garage Sale Millionaire is any individual who searches out those hard-to-find items, hidden gems, or buried treasures, as I like to call them, and turns those found items into a profit. From my experience, not only do Garage Sale Millionaires make money reselling a few choice items, but they usually make very substantial residual profits over time.

Before I even begin to discuss the many ways you, too, can become a successful Garage Sale Millionaire, you should know that one of the most essential elements for success is the ability to have FUN.

What's the point of doing something if you're not totally enjoying yourself? In *How to Become a Garage Sale Millionaire*, I have taken all the mystery and guesswork out of this process, as I show you how to turn everyday items into cold hard cash. Not only will you make some serious money, but you'll also reap a great deal of satisfaction in the process!

Leave behind the boring and mundane at your 9-to-5 job (or jobs) and let's spend some quality time together, as I teach you the ins and outs of collecting, where to find the best collectibles to sell for the most profit, and all the vital information you need to know to strike it rich through buying and selling collectibles.

By the time you've finished reading *How to Become a Garage Sale Millionaire*, you'll be well-equipped with valuable insider knowledge, based on my 40 years of treasure hunting experience. You will have the confidence to know exactly how and where to look for those hidden gems as you strike out on your own to claim your treasure-hunting fortune.

A Treasure Hunter? Is that Really What I Am?

The answer to that question is a definite "Yes." To become a successful Garage Sale Millionaire, you must begin to consider yourself an actual treasure hunter. It takes a treasure hunter's stealth mentality, along with a healthy dose of curiosity, to actively seek out and find that one item, never thought to ever be seen again, that you will be able to turn around and resell for much more than you paid for it.

What is This Book All About?

Within the pages of *How to Become a Garage Sale Millionaire*, collectible-savvy experts will help you navigate the terrain of treasure hunting.

I will personally lead you in the right direction and guide you along the best avenues to travel so that you, too, can turn the pursuit of finding often-overlooked items into money in your pocket. Throughout the pages of *How to Become a Garage Sale Millionaire*, you will gain a wealth of specific, practical knowledge and tremendous insight— insight that can only be gleaned from seasoned collectors, like me, who are willing to share their decades of experience with you. Remember, even in an up, down, or awful economy, there are definite riches to be made!

How to Become a Garage Sale Millionaire is geared specifically towards giving you an advantageous jump on the competition by teaching you how to recognize, and bargain for, those rare, hidden items that are actually treasured finds. Although the collectibles market is highly competitive, I will carefully guide you in your efforts to turn your newfound items into healthy profits. Never in the highly diverse world of collecting has one book covered so many valuable topics, along with an abundance of insider secrets, tips, and tricks for successful treasure hunting

It is my goal to make this book the official go-to guide, and ultimate whenever-you-need-it reference, that you can trust for many years to come. The information presented here is timeless, and will never become outdated. How can that be? *How to Become a Garage Sale Millionaire* is based upon solid treasure-hunting principle acquired from many decades of proven experience.

I offer the proverbial no-stone-unturned approach for you to use in your quest. In the pages to follow, I will give you all the information you will need as you travel down your personal path to becoming a seasoned treasure hunter. I will guide you directly to the unique areas of profit and opportunity that you should seek out when hunting for hidden treasures.

Throughout the years, I've fought my own share of battles to secure those special pieces I just had to have, and now I want to share the wealth of knowledge I've acquired with all of you.

My Pledge to You...

I want you to enjoy this book. So, if you ever have a collection of items you need help with, feel free to contact me.

Whether it's buying or selling, let me know, and I will try to assist you. If you need a good reference for companies to insure, appraise, or even auction items for you, I'm more than happy to help.

Please email me at thegaragesalemillionaire@gmail.com, visit my website, www.thegaragesalemillionaire.com, or check my social media for the newest and best ideas on how you too can make the most out of your new side hustle! You can find me on Facebook, Instagram, and YouTube **@TheGarageSaleMillionaire**

I look forward to hearing from you!

Million $ Tip

While you can't expect to become an expert overnight, you can begin to become more knowledgeable by reading this book. As you begin to build on this foundation with your own personal experience, you will become one of the most knowledgeable treasure hunters around!

CHAPTER 1

Your Garage Sale Millionaire Journey Begins Now!

Even in difficult times, finding consistent monetary success as a treasure hunter is an attainable reality. So, how do you get from Point A to Point B? Point A is where you are now, and Point B, is the point where you are successful at generating income from your treasure-hunting exploits.

Although I was never particularly talented at playing sports, I discovered at an early age how to become exceptional at collecting different items from my favorite athletes. As a kid, I also loved reading comic books and, in fact, I still read them today. Due to my great love for these collectibles, they often drive my treasure-hunting pursuits.

What to collect? Start with something you really like and have a strong interest in. This will ensure that the treasure-hunting process will be much more fulfilling, as well as more profitable, for you. I personally started with specific areas of interest to focus on— certain collectibles I really liked when I was young. This helped set me off on the path to becoming a lifelong collector.

An autographed photo of Thomas Edison given
to my grandfather and then given to me. This
was my very first collectible, and I still
treasure it to this day.

Your Tool Kit

Before you begin your treasure hunt, you'll need a definite plan of action to maximize potential profits. If you're merely collecting items for fun, a serious plan is not important; once you add the goal of making money to the equation, it is required.

There are some basic questions to consider before you can seriously begin your quest to become a Garage Sale Millionaire. Where will you find information —notices for local auctions, item appraisals, or current market trends? How will you process sales and shipments? Through what selling platform? By having all the proper tools and resources at your immediate disposal, you can expedite the selling process and yield a higher return on your invested time. Now, let's discuss those basics, and exactly what weapons you'll need to include in your money-making, Garage Sale Millionaire arsenal.

Million $ Tip

AI like ChatGPT and other great resources can help buyers by analyzing prices, tracking discounts, and recommending the best deals based on preferences and past behavior. It can simplify searches with personalized suggestions and assist in communicating with sellers using chatbots. For sellers, AI can optimize pricing, improve product listings with enhanced images and keyword-rich descriptions, and analyze market trends to attract buyers. It can also automate tasks like inventory management and customer communication, saving time and boosting efficiency. Overall, AI makes online buying and selling faster, smarter, and more profitable.

Your Smart Phone

Any smartphone can be used in place of a digital camera. In addition to being a high-quality camera, your smartphone can be used as a community bulletin board, barcode scanner, personal accountant, and so much more. By taking advantage of the variety of apps available for your smartphone, whether it be an iPhone or Android, you can turn it into any number of useful tools for the field. Here are a few apps that I recommend for selling:

- **eBay**—The eBay app has all of the functionality of the website. It also allows you to instantly create product listings by turning your camera phone into a barcode reader.

- **Nextdoor**—This app functions as a community notice board. Neighbors can share news, recommendations, lost pet notices, and—most importantly for our purposes—advertisements for upcoming garage sales and items for sale. Nextdoor requires address verification to register but will keep you up to date on what's happening close to home.

- **Facebook Marketplace**—This is an online platform within Facebook where users can buy, sell, and trade items locally or across broader areas. It allows individuals and businesses to list products or services, connect with potential buyers or sellers, and negotiate directly through Facebook's messaging system.

- **Craigslist**—Craigslist is an online classified advertisements platform where users can buy, sell, or trade goods and services, as well as post or find job listings, housing, and community events. It operates across various localities worldwide, offering a straightforward, no-frills interface for connecting people within specific geographic areas.

Some great resources to have for buying:

- **All The Local Auction Houses in Your State**—For example, www.shopgoodwill.com is a website that contains all the Goodwill auction items they have up for sale. You can also check for Government auctions on sites like www.govdeals.com or www.usa.gov/auctions-and-sales. Even your city will have local auctions you can find by searching online. When you start to look, it is easy to find even more sites, but this is a good start. FYI—if any apps or sites charge money to download, I would advise against using them.

The best way to get paid or pay someone is through:

- **PayPal**—With PayPal's mobile app, you can securely send, receive and access your money, instantly.

- **Venmo/CashApp**—The Venmo and CashApp mobile apps are another great option for instantly and securely sending and receiving money. If you link your bank account, there are no fees to send or receive payments. If you choose to link your credit or debit card, there will be a service fee.

- **Zelle**—Zelle links through your bank and you can transfer money directly to someone else's bank for no fee. Simply look them up by their phone number or email and you can easily send them money.

> **Million $ Tip**
>
> When using PayPal, Venmo, Zelle, CashApp, etc., be sure to use the friends and family option for sending money if you want to avoid fees.

Most sites and apps that you will use for your treasure-hunting endeavors will be free or low cost.

> **Million $ Tip**
>
> High value items should be listed on eBay or sold through a high-end auction house.

Shipping: Setting Up a Separate Shipping Address and Shipping Account

One of the benefits of having a separate shipping address for conducting your treasure-hunting business is that you can effectively separate your collectible dealings from your personal dealings. Although setting up a separate shipping address is optional and may cost you a nominal fee, it might be the best way to do business.

Setting up a separate shipping address involves renting a mailbox at an established business, such as **The UPS Store** (www.theupsstore.com). Owning a separate mailing address means that you don't have to be present to receive your packages. The store's staff will sign for any shipment and securely store it for you until you come to pick it up. However, there are a couple of negatives involved with this type of arrangement. In addition to a semiannual or annual rental fee for your mailbox, you will have to travel back and forth to pick up items you've purchased or ship items you've sold.

> **Million $ Tip**
>
> Do all of your own packing. Never pay people to pack items for you, as this unnecessary expense will take a big bite out of your profits.

You could consider shipping directly from your home to save money on overhead. If you decide on this option, you need to know that major carriers, such as FedEx and

UPS, require signatures upon delivery for anything of value, and will typically withhold a shipment if no one is available to sign for it. You will need to be present every time a shipment arrives, which could become an issue if you have a full-time job outside of your home.

You will also want to sign up for a shipping account. It is free of charge, and it will help you better manage your records and stay organized. An account can also help you streamline the shipping process, saving time and money; you can save your payment information, schedule pick-ups, and take advantage of member discounts. **The United States Postal Service (USPS)** (www.usps.com), **Federal Express (FedEx)** (www.fedex.com), and **United Parcel Service (UPS)** (www.ups.com) are three of the best companies to consider when securing shipping accounts.

> ## Million $ Tip
>
> You should always take out insurance on whatever you may be shipping, in case something unfortunate happens to it in transit. However, a word to the wise: The United States Postal Service (USPS) has never paid a single one of my claims. This is sad, but true.

FedEx and UPS have the option of managing your deliveries online; you can schedule package pick-ups and reschedule your deliveries if you won't be home. Both companies will also hold shipments at secure locations until you are available to retrieve them. UPS is the best shipping company to choose for high-dollar items over $1,000. FedEx is also a good company, but the insurance limit on collectibles, especially art, is only $1,000. USPS is generally reliable and is usually your most economical option.

When selling on eBay, you do not need to use an outside source. You can print a label right through eBay, and the best part is, that it ends up being cheaper than the rates you'd get going directly through UPS or FedEx.

Million $ Tip

When shipping items valued at more than one hundred dollars, require a signature by the recipient. This will help if porch pirates steal the item that is left on the porch or next to the door of the home. Also, it's always good to send the buyer the tracking number so they can know when the package will arrive.

Cash

Last, but not least, we come to the subject of money... cold, hard cash. Any new venture needs some startup capital, and the business of buying and selling collectibles is no different. The more cash you have access to, the more collectibles you can afford to buy. The math is quite simple: more items to sell equals more profit.

If you don't have much up-front cash set aside for getting started, no problem. There are several other ways to get startup capital together for beginning your new venture. One option is dipping into some of your personal savings; another is to look around your home for items that you can easily afford to part with. Be on the lookout for anything you're not using anymore such as old stereo equipment, unwanted gold or silver jewelry, baby items, used books and videos, computers, coins, or furniture. All of these items can be sold to generate some immediate startup capital.

Whatever you have on hand, and don't need, can be

sold, auctioned off, or offered up at your next garage sale to increase your bankroll. After reading this book, you will be an expert on turning your unwanted items into cash.

Make AI Work for You

Using AI for buying and selling on eBay can significantly enhance your experience by streamlining processes, improving decision-making, and boosting efficiency. For buyers, AI tools can help identify the best deals by analyzing product listings, comparing prices, and monitoring trends. Price-tracking AI can notify buyers when the price of a specific item drops or when a competitive deal is available. Additionally, AI-powered search engines and recommendation systems make it easier to find relevant products by analyzing preferences, past searches, and reviews. Tools like chatbots or virtual assistants can also assist in asking questions to sellers or managing bids effectively, saving time and effort.

For sellers, AI can optimize listing strategies to attract more buyers. AI tools can suggest competitive pricing based on market data and trends, ensuring products are priced attractively without sacrificing profits. Image recognition AI can enhance product photos by removing backgrounds or improving quality, making listings more appealing. Furthermore, natural language processing (NLP) tools can generate optimized product descriptions that include relevant keywords, improving visibility in search results. Sellers can also leverage AI to analyze buyer behavior and feedback, helping tailor marketing strategies or identify potential improvements in their offerings. By automating tasks like inventory management, shipping, and communication with buyers, AI enables sellers to focus on growing their treasure-hunting business efficiently.

CHAPTER 2

To Buy or Not to Buy?
The First Big Question Answered

There's an endless array of items to search for when you're ready to set out on your treasure hunt. For everything that's either manufactured or found in nature, there's usually someone with a desire to collect that particular item. Who knows what will intrigue someone to the point that they say, "I just have to have that!" No matter how odd the item might seem to you, there is indeed someone out there feverishly trying to collect it.

Of course, there are plenty of obstacles that could get in your way, and possibly derail your express journey to Garage Sale Millionaire nirvana. For every item deemed highly collectible, there are items that are not collectible. With literally thousands of collectibles available today, how does someone begin to target an item? What to buy and sell? What not to buy and sell? Which collectibles will make a larger profit for you? More succinctly, how do you find what is valuable and, in turn, what's not? In this chapter, I will give you some ideas, but you can make money off of almost anything if you buy it right.

I've compiled the following list of items that continue to increase in value over the years and will most likely make you the sizable profits you're seeking upon resale Know that these are general guidelines. Before you buy, see what similar items are sold for on eBay. You may be surprised. I have also included those items that have no monetary resale value whatsoever, so you know what to stay away from as well. As you can see, there are many areas from which to collect and many areas you should avoid. As you read through this chapter, I will highlight many of the items found on the list to not only give you a jump on your treasure hunt but also help you maximize the profits from your treasure-hunting adventures.

What to Buy

- Animation Production Cels (High End)
- Antique Bamboo Fishing Poles
- Barbie Dolls
- Trading Cards (Baseball, Football, Basketball, etc.)
- Beatles or Elvis Memorabilia
- Books (Antique or First Edition)
- Civil War Memorabilia
- Coins (American)
- Comics (Pre-1970)
- Depression Glass
- Disney Collectibles
- Fine Art (Research before buying)
- Firearms (Antique)
- Maps (Pre-1700)

- Military Memorabilia (Pre-World War II)
- Motorcycles (Pre-1960 Old Harley Davidsons, Original Indians and Military)
- Movie Memorabilia (Mainly Props)
- Muscle Cars (Pre-1971)
- Pokémon Cards
- Presidential Memorabilia
- Sports Memorabilia (Certified Game Used)
- Stamps (Pre-1920)
- Toy Trains
- Toys (Antique or Tin)
- Toys (Pre-1970, in Original Packaging)
- War Medals (Pre-1900)

What Not to Buy

- Antiques – Only the rare ones hold their value.
- Beanie Babies
- Bibles (Family)
- Foreign Money
- Furs (Old & New)—Nobody wants these.
- Magazines (Old & New)
- Movie Memorabilia (Signed)— There are too many fakes out there.
- Newspapers (Old & New)
- Rugs (Antique - Very Easy to Fake)
- Silverware (Antique & New Silver Plated)
- Sports Memorabilia (Signed)— The market is also too saturated with fakes.
- Stamps (Foreign) Hard to value.

Vice President Gerald R. Ford

*Address Delivered Before a Joint Session of the Congress
on December 6, 1973, Immediately After Taking the Oath of
Office as the 40th Vice President of the United States*

Mr. Speaker, Mr. Chief Justice, Mr. President pro tempore, distinguished guests, and friends:

Together we have made history here today. For the first time we have carried out the command of the 25th amendment. In exactly 8 weeks, we have demonstrated to the world that our great Republic stands solid, stands strong upon the bedrock of the Constitution.

I am a Ford, not a Lincoln. My addresses will never be as eloquent as Mr. Lincoln's. But I will do my very best to equal his brevity and his plain speaking.

I am deeply grateful to you, Mr. President, for the trust and the confidence your nomination implies.

As I have throughout my public service under six administrations I will try to set a fine example of respect for the crushing and lonely burdens which the Nation lays upon the President of the United States. Mr. President, you have my support and my loyalty.

To the Congress assembled, my former colleagues who have elected me on behalf of our fellow countrymen, I express my heartfelt thanks.

As a man of the Congress, let me reaffirm my conviction that the collective wisdom of our two great legislative bodies, while not infallible, will in the end serve the people faithfully and very, very well. I will not forget the people of Michigan who sent me to this Chamber or the friends that I have found here.

Mr. Speaker, I understand that the United States Senate intends in a very few minutes to bind me by its rules. For their Presiding Officer, this amounts practically to a vow of silence. Mr. Speaker, you know how difficult this is going to be for me.

Before I go from this House, which has been my home for a quarter century, I must say I am forever in its debt.

And particularly, Mr. Speaker, thank you for your friendship which I certainly am not leaving. To you, Mr. Speaker, and to all of my friends here, however you voted an hour ago, I say a very fond goodbye. May God bless the House of Representatives and guide all of you in the days ahead.

Mr. Chief Justice, may I thank you personally for administering the oath, and thank each of the Honorable Justices for honoring me with your attendance. I pledge to you, as I did the day I was first admitted to the bar, my dedication to the rule of law and equal justice for all Americans.

For standing by my side as she always has, there are no words to tell you, my dear wife and mother of our four wonderful children, how much their being here means to me.

As I look into the faces that fill this familiar room, and as I imagine those faces in other rooms across the land, I do not see members of the legislative branch or the executive branch or the judicial branch, though I am very much aware of the importance of keeping the separate but coequal branches of our Federal Government in balance. I do not see Senators or Representatives, nor do I see Republicans or Democrats, vital as the two-party system is to sustain freedom and responsible government.

At this moment of visible and living unity, I see only Americans. I see Americans who love their country, Americans who work and sacrifice for their country and their children. I see Americans who pray without ceasing for peace among all nations and for harmony at home. I see new generations of concerned and courageous Americans—but the same kind of Americans—the children and grandchildren of those Americans who met the challenge of December 7, just 32 years ago.

Mr. Speaker, I like what I see.

Mr. Speaker, I am not discouraged. I am indeed humble to be the 40th Vice President of the United States, but I am proud—very proud—to be one of 200 million Americans. I promise my fellow citizens only this: To uphold the Constitution, to do what is right as God gives me to see the right, and within the limited powers and duties of the Vice Presidency, to do the very best that I can for America.

I will do these things with all the strength and good sense that I have, with your help, and through your prayers.

Thank you.

Gerald R. Ford

This was a fun find—a hand-signed vice-presidential signature by Gerald Ford on a pre-printed document. I found it at my local Goodwill store for $16.

What to Buy

I'll let you in on a little secret of mine, so you don't get off track or overly excited when you find something you believe to be of value. Don't be fooled if an item is old or looks expensive. Just because an item is old, doesn't necessarily mean it has any real value. An item that looks expensive could very well be a lesser-valued reproduction or a replica.

Many people see something old and don't understand that there's a lot more to consider than age when determining the value of an item. Sometimes older items are indeed worth money, but age is not the primary factor in assessing a collectible's level of value. For example, a newspaper from July 1969, when American Astronauts first landed on the moon, has no real value. A 200-year-old family bible, although having an emotional value attached to it, also has no market value. However, a 150-year-old empty liquor or spirits bottle could actually be worth over $30,000.

Animation Production Cels

An original animation production cel (short for "celluloid") was created when an artist would draw on celluloid sheets, or "cels," with ink, and then place these cels over painted backgrounds.

In the early years of animation, these cels were made from thin plastic or nitrate, with paint on the back or front of the cel. Each cel represents one frame of a character's movement on film. The animation production cels with the highest collectible resale value are from the late 1920s to the 1960s.

One of the main characteristics to observe in determining an animation production cel's value is whether or not the paint is flaking. A pristine cel will be intact, exhibiting no signs of degradation to the paint. Additionally, these cels can be restored with little value lost.

The other main determinant in verifying the value of an animation cel is the cartoon character depicted. Animation production cels worth the most money upon resale will feature Mickey Mouse, Donald Duck, Bugs Bunny, Bambi, Snow White, or any other main or famous cartoon character. Secondary characters such as Minnie Mouse, Daisy Duck, and Elmer Fudd will not fetch as much money upon resale as their main character counterparts. Additionally, do not let mini-framed prints from **Disney** (www.disney.com) or **Warner Bros.** (www.warnerbros.com) confuse you into believing that they are authentic animation production cels.

Production cels were generally produced in mass amounts. In the early part of the last century, there were usually 24 cels per second, or 60 if you had a smooth look. This means that there could be up to 3600 cels per one minute of animation.

When buying animation cels, the best thing you can look for is limited editions. A limited edition is just that, limited. This means you will find signed editions that generally range from 50 to 750 pieces. Most commonly, 10-12% of additional cels are made as artist proofs and other specialty editions. While cels don't always come with a seal of authenticity, a limited edition will generally always have this seal as well as the number of the work and the edition size. When computers became more sophisticated, they could produce animation at a lower cost. So, while you will find millions of production cells out there, there are smaller collections of originally released limited editions floating around.

A fantastic resource for learning more about cels and their value is *Tomart's Value Guide to Disney Animation Art: An Easy-To-Use Compilation of over 40 Animation Art Auctions Organized by Film, Character and Art Type* by Thomas E. Tumbusch and Bob Wilbaum (1998). This book organizes all Disney animation art sold at major auctions since 1993 by film, character, and type of art. Although it has not been revised or updated in the twenty years since its initial publication, it is still a very useful tool when used in combination with eBay.

Antiques

Antiques are a huge business. How huge? When I search the term "Antique Stores Denver, Colorado", approximately 3,920,000 search results are returned. The same search for "Antique Stores Chicago, Illinois," "New York" and "Los Angeles, California" resulted in about 10,100,000; 28,500,000; and 15,800,000 search results, respectively.

> **Million $ Tip**
>
> Remember, just because one item is older than another, similar item does not mean that more value will be associated with the older item.

When you look at any type of antique furniture—be it desks, chairs, dressers, or sofas—it is extremely important to verify exactly how the item was put together. If the item is a desk or a dresser, check the drawers. Do the drawers match the desk or dresser, or are they additions made well after the original manufacture date of that item? Also, make it a point to check the underside of furniture. This will tell you a great deal about the quality of the item and if it is an authentic antique, a restoration, or a newly manufactured replica. I cover all of this, and more including how you can tell the difference between authentic antiques, fakes, replicas, and restorations, in Chapter 4.

Do be careful with antiques. While there is money to be made, there is also a glut on the market, and prices are falling. Additionally, antiques are hard to ship, which makes them even more difficult to sell.

Barbie Dolls

The Barbie doll was created by inventor Ruth Handler. Since the toy's debut at the 1959 American International Toy Fair in New York City, New York, the Barbie doll has become a collectible phenomenon with tremendous staying power. Barbie doll conventions are held in every major state in the United States, but not in any one state more frequently than once every twenty years.

Barbie dolls made before 1980 have the most collectible resale value of any Barbie doll. As is the case with pretty much every known collectible, the main consideration of the value of a Barbie doll is its condition. Value increases if the original packaging is included with the doll and if it has not been played with very much.

The most valuable among all the Barbies are the pre-1980 dolls still in their original

> **Million $Tip**
>
> Many items from the 1950s through the 1970s have huge collectible value. If you have an item from that period in good condition, with its original packaging, you will have a better than average chance to make more money off that item.

packaging that have never been opened. When collecting Barbie dolls—especially the older, pre-1980 dolls—you will want to make sure the doll comes with all of its accessories and that the original box is in good condition. The absence of the box does not eliminate the value of the piece, but it does play a huge role in retaining or increasing value.

There are several good price guides available for the Garage Sale Millionaire looking to turn a profit buying and selling Barbies. Over the years, I have found eBay, Craigslist, and, at times, garage sales are all great places for finding those Barbie dolls that can be bought and sold for excellent profits.

Bonus trivia: The Ken doll was created in 1961 and was named after Ruth Handler's son.

Beatles & Elvis Memorabilia

Beatles memorabilia has been a popular item to collect since the early 1960s and remains a fantastic collectible area in which to do business for excellent profit! As each year passes, finding authentic Beatles items from the 1960s and 1970s becomes increasingly difficult.

Some Beatles items to look for are old concert tickets, production cels from the cartoon *Yellow Submarine,* posters, figurines, lunch boxes, and vinyl records. To ensure the highest value upon resale, make sure concert tickets are not ripped or torn. One of the most collectible items

> ### Million $ Tip
>
> Unfortunately, for some reason, many items from The Beatles were never properly cared for over the years. If you do find an authentic item from The Beatles in great shape, you can more than likely obtain very good money for it.

from the Beatles catalog includes the infamous "Butcher Block" album cover, with its accompanying vinyl record.

Even the small posters that promoted many of their concerts will net you big money. With regards to tickets and posters, always be wary and keep an eye out for fakes and replicas. You can find Beatles memorabilia on eBay, Craigslist, estate auctions, and, from time to time, at garage sales.

Elvis memorabilia is highly valuable due to the enduring legacy and cultural impact of Elvis Presley, often referred to as the "King of Rock and Roll." As a music icon who revolutionized the entertainment industry, his influence spans generations, making items associated with him deeply sentimental and historically significant. Collectors and fans view Elvis-related artifacts—such as autographs, concert tickets, personal items, and rare recordings—as tangible connections to his life and career. The rarity of authentic memorabilia further drives its value, especially for unique or iconic items like stage-worn outfits or guitars. Auctions for Elvis memorabilia often attract significant attention, with collectors willing to pay premium prices, reflecting both the financial and emotional worth attached to his legendary status.

Books (Antique or First Edition)

To maximize your profits in this collectible category, look for antique books and first editions. **Merriam-Webster** (www.merriam-webster.com) defines the word "antique" as, "Any work of art, piece of furniture, decorative object, or the like, created or produced in a former period, or, according to U.S. customs laws, 100 years before the date of purchase." A first-edition book refers to the first commercial publication of a work.

Why are the first editions of a book so important? First, there may have been only one edition ever published. Secondly, there are normally many changes made to a book between the first and second editions. At times, corrections are made that many authors do not

> **Million $ Tip**
>
> Always buy books in the best condition you can afford. This advice could be applied to any collectible.

acknowledge in subsequent editions. Most importantly, the author may have signed the first edition when promoting the book. So, if you can find a first edition that has been signed, that is a huge coup. Buy it and revel in your good fortune!

How valuable are signed first editions? On October 11, 2002, **Christie's (**www.christies.com**)** auctioned off the first editions of the three *The Lord of the Rings* books by J.R.R. Tolkien, inscribed by the author to his son, Michael. These three first-edition books, *The Fellowship of the Ring* (1954), *The Two Towers* (1954), and *The Return of the King* (1955), sold for $152,500 (Lot 373/Sale 1098). While it is rare for books to command such a high price, consider the fact that even an unsigned first-edition trilogy is currently listed on eBay for $6,500. Let's break down why these books are so valuable: not only are they (1) first editions, but they are also (2) signed by the author, and (3) personally inscribed to the author's son. They belonged in his library, adding ex libris value through a personal connection with Tolkien and his family.

The condition also plays a major role in determining the value of antique books. Before the 1800s, book covers were made of leather and hand-sewn. The better the stitching remains intact on the leather cover, the more valuable the book becomes. Many people have collected antique books for years, yet still do not understand everything there is to know about this type of collectible. There are numerous reference books written on the topic, so before you jump into collecting antique books, I strongly recommend you read a few books on the subject first. Always match the reference books you're considering purchasing with several price guides that cover the same material.

Antique books and first-edition books can be found at garage sales all the time. Estate sales, estate auctions, and eBay are also great places to find antique books. One of the best finds for more recent books is the first edition of Harry Potter. This is a book that I often see at garage sales. Luckily for you, most sellers will not know the actual or true value of the antique books they are selling.

Finding an antique book is actually like finding a diamond in the rough. This is a collectible you could easily find on any given day that could be worth hundreds—if not many thousands—of dollars.

Civil War Memorabilia

I love the subject of history, and I especially love historical memorabilia. Historical memorabilia doesn't get any better than Civil War memorabilia. There are literally hundreds and thousands of items to collect from the American Civil War. If you ever visit Gettysburg, Pennsylvania, you will be amazed at how much Civil War memorabilia is on display and for sale. From this particular conflict, you can collect presidential memorabilia and signed military memorabilia from the likes of Robert E. Lee, Ulysses S. Grant, George Pickett, Joshua Chamberlain, and James Longstreet, plus autographs from numerous well-known and not-so-well-known soldiers. You can also find an abundance of coins and currency, both Union and Confederate, as well a flags, swords, canteens, knapsacks, bottles, pottery, photographs, rifles, guns, artillery, belt buckles, clothes, plates, and drums.

One of my favorite items to collect from the Civil War is diaries. From a historical perspective, diaries are very important because each one includes the personal accounts, thoughts, and actions of that diary's owner. The diary could be from a private, general, sergeant, doctor, or nurse. If this person played a prominent role during the Civil War, the diary would have increased value, in addition to containing a lot of human history within its pages. These diaries will not be cheap—if you can find them. Collectors are beginning to realize how valuable these diaries really are, and they become scarcer every day. A fantastic source for determining the value of Civil War collectibles is *Warman's Civil War Collectibles: Identifying and Price Guide, 3rd Edition* by Russell E. Lee.

Nearly any item from the Civil War era is highly sought after and very collectible. Look for these historical treasures at estate sales, and on eBay and Craigslist.

Coins

Coins are the number one collectible in the United States today. Collectors are always on the lookout for great coin finds. The most important thing to consider with coins is condition. If a gold or silver coin is in poor condition, then the coin is only worth the gold or silver contained in the

> **Million $ Tip**
>
> To make it easier, CoinSnap allows you to take pictures of coins on your phone and gives you a value and background on the items. Many apps now allow you to do this.

alloys of the coin. Also, stay away from foreign coins unless they're made of gold or silver. Foreign coins are only a valuable collectible if you are knowledgeable in that field. I explain about coins and their valuation in much greater detail in Chapter 7.

But first, here are a few key resources you should seek out to gain a better understanding of coins and coin values. The **Professional Coin Grading Service (PCGS)** offers invaluable numismatic information on their main company website (www.pcgs.com), as well as a fantastic online reference tool that you can find at **PCGS Coin Facts** (www.pcgscoinfacts.com). The two best books on coins and coin values are, in my opinion, *The Official "BlueBook" Handbook of United States Coins 2025* by R.S. Yeoman and the official 78th annual edition of *A Guide Book of United States Coins* also by R.S. Yeoman. Both books can be found at your local bookstore or on **Amazon's** website (www.amazon.com).

Comic Books

With comic books, there are a lot more that have value than those that don't. Unfortunately, the condition of most of these comic books is very poor.

Because the majority of older comic books are very valuable, some have been restored to enhance their quality and ultimately their potential resale value. If comics are restored properly, they will retain value quite well. Be mindful and ask about restorations when you find a comic book you want to purchase. The condition is everything, especially when dealing with the buying and selling of comics.

If you find an original comic book illustrated by a

famous comic book artist, that particular book will definitely be worth more money. For this very reason, there are a few comic books made in the last thirty years that have great value as well. Even so, for every new comic book that is valuable, I would say there are hundreds more that have no value whatsoever. To gain a better understanding of which comic book artists are the best in their field, based on each artist's technique, storytelling ability, accomplishments, and longevity, consult "The Top 100 Artists of American Comic Books," a fantastic online resource sponsored by **Atlas Comics** (www.acomics.com/best)

You can use the barcode reader or the reverse image search on eBay to quickly find the value of your comic books. The barcode reader and reverse image search are both inside of eBay and are easy to access on your phone.

Depression Glass

Depression glass refers to glass manufactured between the late 1920s and the early 1940s. From antique guide Pamela Wiggins:

> Manufacturers such as Federal Glass, MacBeth-Evans Glass Co., and Hocking Glass brought a little cheer to some very dreary days by manufacturing the product we now know as Depression glass. This mass-produced molded glassware was of relatively poor quality—often exhibiting air bubbles, heavy mold marks, and other flaws in the glass—yet it came in beautiful colors and patterns to suit every taste. The most popular colors with collectors today are pink in varying hues (some are very light in color, while others have an orange tint to the pink), cobalt blue, and green. Depression glass was also made in

amber, iridescent, opaque white known as Monax, and several other colors as well. Some of the most popular patterns buyers seek today are Cameo, Mayfair, American Sweetheart, Princess, and Royal Lace. Even the pattern names alluded to better times and a longing for the glamorous lifestyles of the 1920s.

Depression glass is also an important collectible for reasons you may not even be aware of. Since the 1960s, it has become much scarcer the older it becomes. An eBay search on "Depression Glass" turned up approximately 57,140 search results for this collectible, with auction prices ranging from $3.00 for a "Federal Depression Glass Spode Dinner Plate" to $2,750 for a "Rare McKee Delphite Poudre Blue 4 Cup Handled Wet Dry Measuring Cup Pitcher." This $2,750 listing is for a very rare measuring cup pitcher made by McKee Glass Company during the Depression, in Delphite blue.

When looking at Depression glass, always use a black light to determine authenticity. A black light, or UV light, is a lamp that emits low levels of electromagnetic radiation, as well as a small amount of little visible light. When American Depression glass is held under a black light, the piece will cast a fluorescent glow. Reproductions of Depression glass, however, will not display any fluorescent properties.

Certain elements within Depression glass absorb invisible light and then discharge that light.

> **Million $ Tip**
>
> A black light is a potent weapon for any Garage Sale Millionaire to use. So, if you are planning on being in this business for a while, you should invest in a black light sooner rather than later.

When this discharge occurs, the glowing effect will be observed. Black lights can be purchased online, with prices ranging from as little as $5 to as high as $400.

Disney Collectibles

In 1928, Walt Disney created his animated masterpiece, Steamboat Willie, featuring the iconic character, Mickey Mouse. From Mickey's humble beginnings, the **Walt Disney Company** (www.thewaltdisneycompany.com) has evolved into a multi-billion-dollar company with theme parks and resorts located all over the world, live-action and animated motion pictures, television shows, stage productions, music industry acts, video games, an amazing amount of consumer products, and the Disney Channel television network.

Because of the Walt Disney Company's amazing popularity throughout the decades, anything produced by Disney has usually been worth very good money. But, since the late 1980s, many items released by Disney have become less than desirable to knowledgeable collectors.

Nowadays, just because an item includes the Disney name, there is no automatic guarantee that there will be a lasting value associated with the item. I've seen many people who think that, because there is a Disney stamp on an item, it is a genuine, properly licensed product from the company. Due to this common misconception, you'll need to do some research before buying any Disney collectible.

So, what are some valuable collectible items from Disney? Pre-1960 animation products from Disney are worth a great deal of money. Many of the classics produced by Disney before 1960 introduce characters beloved around the world—including Mickey and Minnie Mouse, Donald Duck, Pluto, and Goofy. Disney collectibles can easily be found at many garage sales and estate sales and can also be found for sale online through eBay and Craigslist. When you are looking for Disney collectibles, always be aware that there are a great number of people selling these items. You need to know what they are worth before buying anything. There are many great books available about collecting Disney memorabilia. They can be found online and at local bookstores.

If you want to buy and sell Disney collectibles for a profit in your Garage Sale Millionaire endeavors, always make sure you do your research first.

Fine Art

Because I owned a fine art gallery, you could say fine art is my true love. I have a passion for dealing in fine art, animation cels, sports, and entertainment memorabilia, and I work closely with popular artists who regularly have meet-and-greet events at my gallery. I'm not recommending you use the gallery Fascination St. Fine Art as your fine art gallery, but if you're looking to buy art, do find a reputable gallery in your area where you can develop a rapport with the owners and feel comfortable as a customer.

> **Million $ Tip**
>
> When buying art from a fine art gallery, always give the gallery a chance to earn your business. If you like something and feel the price is too high, make them an offer. It never hurts to try. All fair offers made in my gallery are accepted.

I want you to understand that art is a great investment and a great collectible, either to own or resell for future profits. Most of the art you find will already be framed.

Although the frame may look very nice, it could be hiding a multitude of flaws, including physical damage to the piece of art, an incorrectly trimmed edge, or color fading near the perimeter. Any of these defects will greatly diminish the value of the artwork.

Before you spend money on a piece of art, separate the actual artwork from the frame. I will guarantee you that for every 20 pieces you buy and take apart, at least one will have flaws that have been hidden by the frame. Dry mounting the art to a piece of cardboard, foam board, or foam core will eliminate the value of the piece as well unless it is an archival mount. An archival mount consists of an acid-free tissue, coated on both sides with a low temperature, acid-free adhesive.

The acid-free tissue contains an alkaline buffering agent, which neutralizes environmental degradation. A qualified framer can tell you if your art has been mounted using archival standards.

When you're looking for art, whether it's on Craigslist or eBay, in an art gallery, or at a local garage sale, it's important to know the difference between original art, limited edition prints, and a poster of an original piece of art. An original is a piece of art that was completed entirely by the artist. Nothing on the canvas or the artwork's surface was added by anyone other than the artist. A limited-edition print is any work of art that has a fixed number of copies and may or may not be signed. A poster of an original piece of art is simply a poster with the image of an artwork and has little real value. Unless you're an expert, or until you have the piece removed from the frame, it is not always easy to tell the difference. It is a good idea to look at the art without any sort of barrier, such as glass.

Always ask to see the original Certificate of Authenticity (or COA) from the publisher. A Certificate of Authenticity is a document that a gallery or collectibles store gives to the client, which comes from the publisher, guaranteeing the authenticity of the item you want to purchase. Do not accept a COA originated by the gallery or collectibles store and definitely do not accept a COA from someone who just sold you the piece (unless they are the artist's publisher). You must have an original COA from the artist's publisher. This certificate will tell you everything you need to know about the item. Furthermore, make sure you match the number on the COA with the number on the piece of art. If the numbers don't match, then ask the fine art gallery for the matching certificate. If they cannot provide one, you may have to rethink your purchase decision and pass on the item.

When buying from a non-gallery venue, such as a collectibles store, the process is still the same. Always make certain to ask for the original COA. If the retailer does not have the original certificate, either rethink your purchase or have your local gallery advise you on the item in question. A local fine art gallery will usually appraise or certify a piece for a nominal fee, or even for free if they are going to re-frame the item for you. I discuss Certificates of Authenticity in Chapter 4 in greater detail.

If your piece of art is damaged and the artist is still alive, there is a chance you can have your local gallery call the publisher directly so that they can replace the piece of art for a small fee. If you picked up the art piece for a cheap price and it's damaged, there is a good chance you can get the piece of art replaced. What actually happens when it's replaced? The publisher takes your damaged piece of art, destroys it, reprints it, and renumbers it with the exact number you originally had. The publisher then has the artist sign the new item. This common practice is completely legitimate, totally acceptable, and is not considered fraud. What you've really just done is purchase a brand-new piece of art for one-tenth of what that same piece would have cost when it was brand new. Of course, this does not work if the item you have is an original, as an original work of art can never be duplicated. You should always be absolutely certain that there is no damage to an original artwork you are interested in before you purchase it.

When you walk into a gallery and purchase an item, you're paying a premium to buy from that gallery, but there are tremendous benefits to be derived from doing so. There's a lot you can learn from a fine art gallery owner about the art business. By doing business with a gallery, no matter how small the item you purchase, a smart owner will do whatever is necessary to keep you as a client. The gallery owner or staff can also help you by answering questions and may become a valuable resource for you in the future.

Firearms (Antique)

This is an incredible collectible. There is a better-than-average chance you will not see antique firearms being sold at your local garage sale, but there are numerous antique firearm auctions held across the country throughout the year. For firearm auctions in your area, investigate listings online or at local gun shops.

Savvy collectors know that when an antique firearm is not in working order its value will decrease slightly, but that particular firearm may still be a very collectible item and could net an excellent profit upon resale. Overall condition is another factor in determining an antique firearm's market value. Does the firearm have any rust? Is it corroded? If a gun is heavily rusted, noticeably corroded, or the wood on the gun is seriously marred, the value will be reduced substantially.

It is important to know that the buying and selling of firearms falls under the jurisdiction of the **Bureau of Alcohol, Tobacco, Firearms and Explosives (or the ATF)** (www.atf.gov). What does this mean for you?

When you purchase a firearm, it's illegal for you to transport that firearm across state lines. So, you need to be very cautious when you are buying or selling any weapon. I do need to clarify something, concerning antique firearms. If a firearm doesn't use a type of ammunition that's currently available, for example, uses black powder, you will be able to transport and ship the gun yourself. It is only when a firearm takes ammunition that is currently on the market that you cannot ship or transport it across state lines.

If you find a modern gun you really want to purchase, you need to locate an authorized gun dealer in the area where the sale is taking place and have them transport the piece across state lines. Whenever you're buying a firearm, there is also a better-than-average chance you will have to apply for either a gun permit and/or obtain clearance from the state in which you legally reside allowing you to possess a gun. If you are unsure of your state's gun laws, contact the ATF or your local police department. Yes, there are certain hurdles you must overcome when you want to own a firearm, but the

---

Million $ Tip

The entertainment industry produces many replica guns for movies and television shows. Many of these fake weapons are available for sale, in some stores alongside actual firearms.

benefits—in the form of potential profits, if you want to resell an antique firearm—certainly make it worth your while.

In antique firearms, the biggest and most recognized names are **Winchester Ammunition** (www.winchester.com) and **Colt Manufacturing** (www.colt.com). Weapons made by Colt have played a part in every war involving the United States since the mid-1800s. The Colt revolver, invented by company founder Samuel Colt, is known by many historians as the "gun that won the West". The most valuable Colts were manufactured between the mid-1800s and the turn of the 19th century. The value of a particular Colt firearm may also be dependent upon the role it played in any given conflict.

The best Winchesters to deal in for-profit were made during the late 1800s when the western United States was still the Wild West. These antique guns are of considerable value if they are in very good condition. Once again, the condition of any collectible item plays a huge role in determining proper value.

In terms of antique firearms, anything pre- 1893 will have a higher value and will be easier to buy and sell. When purchasing antique firearms, always be cognizant that there are a lot of replicas that intricately copy old rifles and handguns. If the condition of an antique firearm is too good to be true, it's a good sign that the item may be a replica or a reproduction.

There are many great books on this topic available at your local library or from your local bookstore. The internet is also a great resource to tap into for learning more about this subject. I recommend you become as knowledgeable as possible about this collectible before you attempt to buy an antique firearm.

Military Memorabilia (Pre-World War II)

Military memorabilia prior to World War II will make you the most profit in this area of collectibles. World War II, the Korean War, and Vietnam-era items have less overall value because, from a historical perspective, these wars are considered too recent. I say this solely from a monetary viewpoint. There is, of course, an unbelievable amount of emotional value and emotional currency placed on memorabilia from these conflicts, as these wars were unquestionably important to many individuals, to the United States of America, and to American history.

The hierarchy of military memorabilia acquisitions, based solely on monetary value is, first, the Civil War, followed by the Revolutionary War, World War I, and World War II. Any collectible related to the Nazis is difficult to address, due to the psychological wounds and deep social resonance that continues to affect an amazing number of individuals worldwide. Although you may be able to find Nazi memorabilia being sold by private dealers, this type of collectible is generally not allowed on eBay or in many auction ads. If you come across an authentic Nazi item to purchase, it will indeed be collectible, but you may have a difficult time trying to make a return on your investment for the foreseeable future.

As I discussed earlier in this chapter, Civil War memorabilia is extremely collectible. A few specific items I would seek out are Civil War diaries, weapons, uniforms, and flags. All these items are highly sought after by col- lectors. If you come across a good deal, you might want to purchase a few pieces. Between Civil War movies—such as *Gettysburg, Gods and Generals,* and *Glory*—and Civil War reenactments, which take place throughout different parts of the United States, there are many Civil War replicas available for sale. Most memorabilia dealers selling these types of items acknowledge the fact that some of their wares are replicas, but many people are not so forth- coming with that information. Often, it is difficult to tell the real thing from the fake. Pre-1893 military weapons are also highly collectible. Guns from Winchester Ammunition, called Winchesters, were used during the Civil War, or to "tame the Wild West," and they are very valuable. Muskets and handguns from the Civil War and Revolutionary War are highly sought after as well.

You could easily overpay for many of these items, so be very aware of what you are purchasing. There is a multitude of books written on this topic in addition to extensive information available on the internet. So, before you dive into this collectible, make sure you thoroughly research the topic.

Motorcycles (Pre-1960 Old Harley-Davidsons, Original Indians, and Military)

Even though I personally enjoy motorcycles, my wife does not allow me to ride them anymore. Of course, the next best thing to riding motorcycles is collecting them. Military motorcycles and motorcycles manufactured before 1960—including models from historical American motorcycle manufacturing companies, such as **Harley-Davidson USA** (www.harley-davidson.com) and **Indian Motorcycles** (www.indianmotorcycle.com)—are the most desirable for collectors to buy.

The number one name in motorcycles is, hands down, Harley- Davidson; original Indian Motorcycles follow as a close second. The maker of Indian Motorcycles has gone bankrupt several times since their founding in 1901 but, in the late 1940s and 1950s, they were a very serious player in the motorcycle manufacturing business. Unfortunately, not many Indian Motorcycle bikes exist today. They were not manufactured in large quantities due to the company's numerous financial problems and bankruptcies through the years. Because finding a vintage Indian Motorcycles bike is a rare occurrence, they are extremely valuable to collectors.

Early Harley-Davidsons, or old military motorcycles from the 1930s and 1940s, are also a very big deal. Many of these older motorcycles will be badly rusted, and in poor to very poor condition when/if you come across them. If you do manage to find an old Harley, Indian, or military motorcycle in a state of disrepair, don't worry. The condition really doesn't matter that much—the rarity of finding just one of this type of collectible more than makes up for any deterioration. These are always very valuable finds.

When you visit a prospective seller's home and speak with them about their collectible, always ask about motorcycles. If people have an old barn or garage that looks like no one has gone through it in a while, make sure to inquire (politely) about what might be stored inside. You could just be the one person to find that missing original Indian Motorcycles, or that one hard-to-find classic Harley-Davidson no one has been able to discover over the decades. The worst anyone can say is, "No". If you do happen across one of these bikes, quickly think of a way to get this valuable find off their hands. Negotiate a fair purchase price, buy the item, and have it moved immediately before someone else does.

Congratulations! You have just put yourself in a prime

position to potentially make a lot of money when you re-sell. Believe me when I tell you that scenario occurs every day with real Garage Sale Millionaires across the country. With a little curiosity and perseverance, it could also happen to you!

Movie Memorabilia (Mainly Props)

Movie props hold immense value because they provide a tangible connection to iconic films, characters, and moments that have left lasting impressions on audiences worldwide. The rarity and authenticity of movie props further elevate their value. Many props are one-of-a-kind or produced in limited quantities, particularly for high-budget films where attention to detail is paramount. Once a production wraps, props are rarely replicated, making their availability finite. Authenticity, verified through certificates or provenance, adds another layer of exclusivity, assuring collectors they are purchasing a genuine piece of cinematic art. This rarity, combined with the cultural and nostalgic significance of the film, drives demand and often results in competitive bidding at auctions.

The investment potential of movie prop memorabilia also contributes to its value. As the popularity of certain films or franchises grows over time, so does the worth of items associated with them. Memorabilia from cult classics, superhero films, or award-winning blockbusters often appreciates in value, appealing not only to fans but also to investors. Furthermore, the public display of movie props in museums or exhibitions amplifies their prestige, turning them into symbols of cultural heritage. In this way, movie props transcend their original purpose, becoming cherished artifacts that celebrate the art of filmmaking and its impact on society.

Muscle Cars (Pre-1971)

When searching for muscle cars during your many collectible treasure hunts, you will most likely not see these kinds of cars at your local garage sale.

But, with the help of **Barrett-Jackson Car Auctions** (www.barrett-jackson.com), **M e c u m Auto Auctions** (www.mecum.com) and **Fox Motor Sports** (www.foxmotorsports.com), acquiring muscle cars has come to the forefront of the American collecting scene. Muscle cars are defined as American, mid-size cars, manufactured from 1964 to 1972, that were enhanced with large, powerful V8 engines, superchargers, and special exhaust systems. The first true muscle car was the 1964 Pontiac GTO, a car immortalized forever with the release of the mega-hit record "Little GTO" by Ronny & the Daytonas. The most valuable muscle cars to buy and sell for profit were manufactured before 1971.

Because we're discussing the subject of cars and, more specifically, muscle cars, I'm sure you understand that golden oldies like these cannot be purchased for $50, $100, or even $1000. Muscle cars are going to cost you much more! I want you to keep an open mind about this type of collectible. Why? Because you can make substantial sums of money buying and selling muscle cars. Pre-1971 muscle cars are generating huge sales with an enormous return on investment. Fords, Buicks, and Corvettes (with big block engines), or anything with a Hemi, carry an extremely high value. A Hemi, if you're wondering, is an extremely powerful, internal- combustion engine.

Most people underestimate the money-making potential involved in buying and selling muscle cars. For example, a restored 1965 Mustang Convertible recently sold for $100,000 in a 2021 Barrett Jackson Auto

Auction in Houston, Texas. According to the **Henry Ford Museum Archive** (www.thehenryford.org/collections-and-research/digital-collections/artifact/332010), when the 1965 Ford Mustang was released, the vehicle cost approximately $3,334, making the difference a staggering $96,666. If you calculate for inflation, $3,334 in 1965 would equate to about $32,250 today, which is still an astounding difference of $67,750. If you were lucky enough to have purchased this car back in 1965, and you sold it at auction in 2021, this could have been your profit. Not everyone is holding onto a great classic muscle car that they bought back in the '60s, but there are many opportunities to find cars in great condition that can be sold for a profit.

The overall condition of any muscle car is very important to consider if you want to resell it with the least amount of effort and for the most profit possible. To determine a muscle car's condition, check to see if there is rust or corrosion on the vehicle, verify if all the parts on the car are original, and ensure that the Vehicle Identification Numbers (VIN) on the car's engine block match the VIN on the main frame of the car. Also, try to get all the information you can from the current owner of the car. If you ever find a vehicle that has only one owner, and he or she has documentation to accompany the car, it will add huge value to the vehicle

When gathering information on any muscle car you have a strong interest in purchasing, try to find out where the vehicle was primarily operated or housed geographically. If the muscle car came from the middle portion of the United States, the Midwest, the vehicle would more than likely have greater value. This is because of salt in the environment. Salt is the archenemy of muscle cars. The reason you want to be careful when purchasing a muscle car from a coastal region is the salt in the air.

Over time, salt in the air can cause a great deal of damage to a car that you may or may not be able to see. Salt will destroy anything metallic on a car, from its exterior finish to any part under the hood. Even though I have identified salt as being a problem primarily for states bordering massive bodies of water, salt can also be trouble in snowy regions, where salt is widely used on roads to help melt ice. If a muscle car was driven during a harsh Midwestern winter, there could be salt corrosion and rust on the vehicle.

If a muscle car has all of its original parts intact, as well as the original interior upholstery and original external paint, then the resale value of the vehicle will be much higher. If you find a car that has been restored and re-painted, the restoration will not diminish the value of the car, as long as it has been done properly. Many muscle cars that sell at auto auctions, such as the Barrett-Jackson Car Auctions and Mecum Auto Auctions, have been meticulously restored, or even subject to a full rotisserie restoration.

A rotisserie restoration is when a car is completely disassembled, and the body is taken off the vehicle's frame. Next, the body of the vehicle is placed on a rotisserie, which can be turned to show any area of the car. From this point, the body of the car can be sandblasted to bare metal, have body work completed, and be primed, painted, and reassembled in exactly the same way the vehicle was originally manufactured at the factory. Just remember, if an automobile restoration has been rendered, make sure that restoration was done properly.

Muscle cars offer the Garage Sale Millionaire a chance to make a larger amount of money when compared to other collectibles. Always do your research before you make any purchasing decisions. By doing this, you'll be ahead of your competitors when it comes to buying and selling muscle cars for a substantial profit.

Pokémon Cards

Pokémon cards have become one of the most sought-after collectibles to date. Some of these cards, in good condition, and certified with a grade, can go for tens of thousands of dollars. When you find these cards while you are out and about treasure hunting, inspect them very carefully. You can refer to the four criteria that I talk about late in Chapter 7, but the gist of it is, you want to look for cards that look perfect. You want to avoid anything with any kind of creasing. If the corners are bent or dented, that's also a no go.

Pokémon cards are highly valuable due to their nostalgic appeal, rarity, and the enduring popularity. For many, these cards represent a cherished part of childhood. Certain cards, especially those from the early sets or limited-edition releases, are exceedingly rare, with values determined by their condition, edition, and availability. Competitive play also adds to their worth, as high-value cards often hold strategic importance in the game. The market for Pokémon cards has surged in recent years, with high-profile sales and media attention further boosting their status as collectibles and investments. For example, Jake Paul (a famous YouTuber) traded a PSA 10 Grade Pikachu Illustrator Card that set him back $5,275,000.

If you can find these cards in good condition, there's a good chance you can rake in some serious cash if you get them authenticated.

Posters (Pre-1977, Movie and Music)

If you love to collect movie and music posters, don't pay extra for posters with authentic signatures unless they are verified by a regulated agency, such as **James Spence Authentication** (www.spenceloa.com). I talk about James Spence Authentication, or JSA, in more detail in Chapter 4. Signatures verified through JSA have already been certified as genuine, so you're not just taking a store owner's word that the signature is authentic. This is very important when you're ready to spend a sizable amount of money on that one poster you believe to be very valuable. Pre-1977 posters from the movie and music business are the most collectible.

Million $ Tip

Signed movie and music posters are two of the most of- ten, and most easily, faked items in the history of memorabilia collecting. It is extremely difficult to verify and/ or document that the actual movie stars or musicians signed the posters. My recommendation is not to collect these items. They are fun to have, but don't pay big money for them unless you have them certified authentic.

Sports Memorabilia (Certified Game-Used)

To be placed in the game-used category, a sports memorabilia item must have been used in an actual sporting event. Game-used sports memorabilia needs to be properly documented with a Certificate of Authenticity, which could come from the team, the player who used the item during the game, or a certifying agency.

I traded Claude Lemieux a box of Cuban Cigars for his Game Worn Avalanche Jersey.

Certification is very important because, without it, the item is just a piece of used sports equipment with no significance attached to it. If the game-used item does not come from a famous athlete or was not used during an important game, such as the Super Bowl, World Series, or Stanley Cup Finals, then the item will be worth less money. Game-used sports memorabilia's condition is not as important as the player who used the item, so long as it is documented through proper certification of authenticity.

Besides a Certificate of Authenticity from a reputable dealer, people are demanding photos that match the athlete to the sports item. With that, you can match up the tears, stains, scuffs, etc. allowing you to be sure that the item was actually used in an athletic event.

Stamps (Pre-1920)

I distinctly remember collecting stamps and coins when I was a child. But to me, stamps were far more fun than coins. With stamps, there was always a cool color picture, and every stamp had a different story to tell. I've had great fun collecting stamps over the years, but I must share that stamp collecting is the worst collectible you can be involved in. Why? Because there have been millions upon millions of stamps manufactured over the years and, as a result, many stamps retain zero collectible value. Another reason for stamps being an undesired collectible is, if stamps are canceled, that post-office stamp (yes, a stamp on a stamp) eliminates any kind of value the stamp may have had. First-day stamp covers also hold very little value.

I know what you're thinking: "Why, then, did you list stamps as something in the What to Buy column if you believe they are the worst collectible you can be involved in?" Although many stamps have no monetary value, stamps that originated before 1920, and have no cancellation stamp from the United States Post Office, are quite collectible.

The only exception to the non-cancellation rule is if the stamp is dated pre-1800. With these early stamps, cancellation will not harm the value.

Some stamps are, indeed, quite valuable. If you decide to begin the treasure hunt for this type of collectible, you really need to thoroughly understand how to value stamps. I suggest you get a copy of *The Official Blackbook Price Guide to United States Postage Stamps* by Thomas E. Hudgeons, Jr.

ToyTrains

Toy trains are a very entertaining collectible to become involved with. They have a rich history and have proven to be an extremely profitable collectible to trade in as well. Although **Lionel Trains** (www.lionel.com) will be the number one recognized brand as you search for toy trains, there are many other manufacturers, such as **American Flyer** (www.americanflyertrains.com) and **Bachmann Industries** (www.bachmanntrains.com), both have made classic and collectible toy trains over the years. Individual toy train cars, complete locomotive sets, and entire toy train villages are consistently resold for amounts ranging from just a few cents to tens of thousands of dollars.

Condition and packaging are extremely important factors in determining the value of any collectible, and toy trains are no different. The better condition the train is in, along with its original packaging, the more money the train will generate upon resale. Additionally, some toy trains and toy train sets may have been restored. If restoration has taken place, the value will drop. When you buy a very old toy train, examine it closely to make certain your item hasn't been restored and isn't missing any parts.

Trading Cards (Baseball, Football, Basketball, etc.)

Even though trading cards are a highly sought-after collectible item, many of these collectibles have little or no real value. Three factors will affect the value of any trading card: the condition of the card, the card's age, and the historical significance of the player featured on the card. If the trading card is a rookie card of a great player, then it will be worth more money. Trading cards that have increased in value over the past few years either have a player's signature included on the card or have a piece of the player's jersey in the card.

A great way to enhance or increase the value of a card is to have the trading card professionally graded. A professional grade on a trading card could add up to 40% to its value, and the fee for such a service only costs approximately $15 to $25 per card. There are several certified companies that professionally grade cards. I discuss grading trading cards in great detail in Chapter 7.

If you want to easily look up the value of a trading card, you can use the app **CardBase** (www.getcardbase.com). CardBase allows you to scan the trading card and find it within their database. The app will show all the card's information along with an estimated price that the card could be worth. You can log your trading card collection in the app and it will even send you notifications when a card that is in your collection increases or decreases in value. This app does require a paid subscription.

Vinyl Records

For vinyl records or vinyl record album covers to have any real value, they need to be packaged together. If you're looking to make any serious money from these collectibles, you simply cannot have one without the other. For example, if you have a record without its associated album cover, there will be no value attached to that vinyl record. Likewise, if you have an album cover without its associated record, little to no value will relate to that item. Although vinyl record album covers made before 1977 retain the highest value, this doesn't necessarily mean vinyl records have to be from this era to be valuable.

Condition is considerably important in determining value. Many old album covers, especially from records produced by mega-popular bands like The Beatles and the Rolling Stones, may be deemed highly collectible if they are original. However, do watch out for restored covers! If an album cover has been restored, it loses some of its value and loses ALL value if done poorly. This type of item is well worth collecting, but you must be highly observant and knowledgeable on the subject to make a profit.

Although digital downloads have taken over the lion's share of today's audio market, vinyl records have been making a comeback in recent years. Record Store Day continues to grow in popularity each year, with more and more titles becoming available. Record Store Day 2024, held on April 20, significantly boosted vinyl sales, contributing to the highest weekly total in 30 years.

Vinyl records may still be considered a niche market, but those who continue to invest in turntables and stereo equipment that costs thousands, tens of thousands, or even hundreds of thousands of dollars are extremely passionate about their hobby. These impassioned collectors spare no expense in seeking out and buying the best vinyl available to play on their tricked-out, two-channel audio systems.

It's a point of contention among those who enjoy listening to music in a digital format—as in digital downloads and compact discs—and those who prefer listening to music in analog format, via vinyl records, as to which sounds better and more authentic.

On vinyl record auction results websites, such as **Popsike** (www.popsike.com), there are tens of thousands of vinyl record auction results listed. Vinyl records from groups, solo artists, and composers—ranging from the

Beatles to Beethoven, Bob Dylan to Elvis Presley, and from Queen to Velvet Underground—can fetch upwards of $20,000-$25,000, or more, per album. You can also use the app **Discogs (**<u>www.discogs.com</u>**)** to find values on vinyl, as well as catalog your collection, explore music, buy music, track your want list, and more. Although most vinyl records may not have a lot of resale value, older vinyl records from important, ground-breaking individuals or groups in the music industry command substantial amounts of money upon resale.

Thrift stores are great places to look for vinyl records, as are second-hand stores, vinyl record stores, and, of course, garage sales. When you find an old vinyl record, you need to check the condition of the record to see that no scratches are present. You'll also want to make sure the sleeve is intact and undamaged. Most importantly, check price guides to see if what you're holding is valuable. Websites like eBay and Popsike, as well as books, such as *The Official Price Guide to Records, 18th Edition* by Jerry Osborne, and *Goldmine Record Album Price Guide: The Ultimate Guide to Valuing Your Vinyl, 10th Edition* by Dave Thompson, are valuable tools in determining if the record you hold in your hands will be worth any money upon resale.

What Not to Buy

We now transition to those collectibles that should be avoided at all costs. Sir Isaac Newton once said, "For every action, there is an equal and opposite reaction." This quote directly relates to the following section of this book.

As great as the previously mentioned collectibles are concerning money-making potential, what follows is a detailed description of the equal and opposite collectibles that are not worth your time. Dealing with the following collectibles will do one thing and one thing only: waste your time and money.

Beanie Babies

The number one fad collectible of all time—and, quite possibly, the worst collectible of all time—is, in my opinion, the Beanie Baby. A fad collectible is an item that, when released for sale, is extremely popular. A better description would be that the popularity of most fad collectibles starts off the charts—the masses go crazy for them upon their release. Because of the overwhelming initial interest they create, fads attract many collectors who assume interest guarantees lasting value.

After the initial excitement subsides, the collectible eventually loses almost all its importance and is left with no real value. I can't tell you the number of people, including seasoned businessmen, who hopped on the Beanie Baby bandwagon and started collecting them when they were first introduced in 1993 by **Ty Warner Inc. (now Ty, Inc.,** www.ty.com**).**

Beanie Baby collectors were obsessed with amassing these pellet-filled, stuffed animal toys that are virtually worthless in today's collectibles market, some even spending tens of thousands of dollars along the way. To this day, Beanie Babies are one collectible that has everybody fooled.

Experience has shown me that whenever a collectible soars quickly, chances are good it will plummet just as fast.

Bibles (Family)

There is no opportunity for financial gain in buying or selling family Bibles unless the bible comes from a famous family. The average family bible does not have any resale value. Although a family bible may have personal importance to your own family, it will not mean anything to someone else.

Magazines (Old & New)

I know many people who collect old magazines. My mom saved old *National Geographic* magazines and believed with all her heart that her stash of *Nat Geos* would set me up for life if I ever needed to sell them. With old magazines such as *National Geographic, Time, Life,* and *The New Yorker,* it's difficult to find copies with collectible value. There are, however, a few exceptions to the rule.

A magazine's premier issue could potentially be valuable. The very first issue of *Playboy,* published in December of 1953 with Marilyn Monroe on the cover, is the most valuable of any *Playboy* and can command sales of several thousand dollars. In addition to its first edition, *Playboy* has a few issues dating from the 1950s and '60s that have true lasting value as well, particularly if the copies are in pristine condition. With *National Geographic, Time,* and *Life,* among others, there may be something on the cover that makes an issue very rare, but looking for these magazines is like finding a needle in a haystack. I would stay far away from this collectible because any upside opportunities are quite limited.

Movie Memorabilia (Signed)

Movie memorabilia is wonderful to collect, but you need to be aware that signed movie memorabilia is associated with a great deal of fraud. Many of the signatures and autographs used to sell this kind of movie memorabilia are often verified as fakes. When you're buying a signed piece of movie memorabilia from that famous movie star you absolutely adore, do be aware that the chances of the item having been signed by that particular person are slim to none.

Signatures on movie memorabilia are extremely hard to verify unless you take your item to a company like **James Spence Authentication** (www.spenceloa.com) to professionally certify your item as authentic. I cover the topic of movie memorabilia in more detail in Chapter 4.

Newspapers (Old & New)

Whenever I speak to an audience, or when I'm interviewed on the radio or television, people always ask about old newspapers. Unfortunately, the value of old newspapers is like stamps. Because there were tens of thousands, if not millions, of newspapers printed over the years, many have very little value. Their condition is also unstable. They tend to yellow very quickly, and storing them together exacerbates the yellowing process, so finding a newspaper in good to pristine condition is extremely difficult.

If you want to talk about newspapers that may have considerable value, you'll need to go back to those printed in the 1800s. Try to look for newspapers dating historically close to the time when President Abraham Lincoln was assassinated (1865). If you find a newspaper you think has value, you want to take care of it right away by placing it in a protective plastic cover. Like old magazines, this collectible has very little upside.

Rugs (Antique)

Authentic antique rugs have great value, but this is another specialized collectible area in which you must be an absolute expert if you are to determine what's valuable and what's not. This collectible item also demands that you have an expert in your corner. You need someone with experience, someone you can completely trust to buy your rugs for you. Even if you work with a professional, experienced rug dealer, you can still be misled with antique rugs because there are a great many replica rugs manufactured, easily posing as authentic and antique.

> **Million $ Tip**
>
> When verifying authenticity, look at the knots that hold the rug together. High-end carpets have 500 knots per square inch. If the knots are uneven or the pattern is off-center, it is highly likely that the rug is handmade. Carpets made after 1920 were usually made by machines.

This collectible can be very expensive and, if you're not an expert yourself, or you don't work with a reputable expert, I can almost guarantee you're going to lose a lot of money.

Antique rugs are a difficult-to-learn collectible that takes a great deal of time to understand.

Million $ Tip

To test authenticity, you can take a few small pieces of a rug's fabric and light them on fire. Then, look at the color of the flame. If there is color present (other than the color of a normal flame, that is), then you know you have a newer, machine-made carpet. Of course, always use the utmost caution when working with fire to avoid any accidents!

Silverware (Antique)

Pure silver was never used in antique silverware because it is actually too soft of metal unless mixed with other alloys. All antique silverware was produced with different types of metals along with pure silver. Antique silverware is collectible, but now it's mainly desirable for the potential amount of silver these items physically contain. It only holds the silver weight value, not any real value.

There were a few early manufacturers—such as Gorham, Whiting, Towle, Dominick & Haff, Reed and Barton, R. Blackinton & Co., Tiffany, Unger Bros., and Wallace—who created silverware that has maintained some lasting value throughout the years. Finding antique silverware may pose challenges due to the rarity of more valuable pieces. You want to become very knowledgeable about antique silver before you buy.

Don't get overly excited when you find some antique silver at an antique store or a garage sale that you think is undervalued. Do your homework before you make any purchase. Make sure you verify whether the piece of silverware is sterling silver or silver-plated.

Many times, people think that just because a piece is old it's going to be sterling silver. Silver plating was used much more commonly than most people think, so be mindful of this fact before you buy.

Million $ Tip

As a rule, antique silverware will always be worth no less than the amount of actual silver contained in each piece. If you are only interested in an item for its silver content, great. If not, you will need to find more information before buying anything in this area of collectibles. Sterling silver is 92.5% pure silver. The remaining percentage is an alloy, combined with silver to make the metal stronger. Most sterling silver items will have a stamp or hallmark on the bottom of the item.

Also, look for the hallmark, maker's mark, or stamp on the underside of the item. Stamps are usually found on the backside of cutlery. Look for these marks on the neck, where the sharp edge meets the handle of a fork, knife, or spoon. With tea sets, marks are always on the underside of the pieces. Most of the pieces should have some form of mark on them, which will tell you who manufactured the item, as well as the percentage of silver it contains.

If you don't have the proper knowledge of what is collectible and what isn't, that pricey antique tea set you're thinking of purchasing for its potential resale value may not be worth as much as you think.

Sports Memorabilia (Signed)

Sports memorabilia can really be as exciting and challenging as the sport itself. But, like anything else in the world of collectibles, you must always be cautious when verifying that an item is authentic. When you're thinking of purchasing a piece of sports memorabilia, always ascertain that the item has been certified by one of the major certification companies, such as **James Spence Authentication** (www.spenceloa.com), **The Upper Deck** (www.upperdeck.com), or **Steiner Sports** (www.steinersports.com), among others you can search online for.

Additionally, due to the popularity of eBay, there are many well- done fakes and forgeries. These items are mass-produced by a skilled cadre of sellers to make a quick buck. I estimate that for every one authentic signature, there are probably two that are forged. For a piece to have any true value, you need to have it certified by a well-known certification company, such as those mentioned previously in this section. I will cover this topic in more detail in Chapter 4.

Stamps (Foreign)

It would be best if you stayed as far away as possible from foreign stamps. Yes, like everything else in this world, there will always be a few exceptions to the rule. You could possibly find a few foreign stamps with some value but, from my experience, there aren't many out there. Even if someone is selling one hundred thousand stamps on eBay for just $100, it will take you an incredibly long time to find that one stamp that is worth a few dollars. It takes too much time and effort to discover even a few stamps that might eventually have some value.

Again, this is one collectible I would recommend staying away from altogether. When you're offered a great deal on foreign stamps, although the deal may be tempting, I'm telling you, trust me on this: run as fast as you can in the opposite direction!

Million $ Tip

Never buy international stamps if you're hoping to make money. Their only value is to people who are experts in this field.

"To Buy or Not to Buy?" That is the Question!

In this chapter, I described many categories of items you will encounter daily as you foray out on your adventurous treasure hunts. When you come across a piece that interests you, you'll need to determine if it falls under the category of What to Buy, or if it falls under the category of What Not to Buy.

Eventually, you'll find one particular item that intrigues you so much you're moved to start collecting it. When you find one collectible that's right for you and you want to start buying and selling, read everything you can about that item. Strive to become an expert in that collectible.

Thoroughly research your interests and re-read this book. And always remember, there is much to learn and great fun to be had in educating yourself about your specific collectible.

Often, when you first begin collecting one item, such as antiques or fine art, you will most likely become interested in collecting other items in different genres. You may eventually pursue something far different, in an area you never imagined could hold your attention. When you become a Garage Sale Millionaire, you need to be knowledgeable in several different collectibles. Why? So, when you go to garage sales, auctions, storage unit auctions, and estate sales—or when you buy and sell items via the internet— you'll be prepared to purchase items to sell for a profit.

In this chapter, when I say a collectible has no value, please understand that I am generalizing. For every Beanie Baby, foreign stamp, or new fad collectible, there will be a few items that will still have value to some buyers somewhere.

Also, no matter how often I say an item is something you should not buy, there usually exists a collector who will be looking feverishly to collect that exact item.

Most importantly, be careful throughout the course of your Garage Sale Millionaire adventures. I would rather you err on the side of caution, because the overall collectible category either has a bad reputation or at other times, it may be that you're trying to purchase that one hard-to-find item in an entire collectible category that simply has no value.

For all the details I've shared in this chapter, I have merely scratched the surface of the collectibles market. As always, there are many great collectibles to be bought and sold for substantial profit.

An Eyvind Earle Original on Board that I procured from eBay for $3,000, which was an amazing deal. People really don't know the value of things, so if you spend time looking at a lot of things on eBay you will end up finding good deals like this one. This piece This piece ended up being valued at $25,000.

CHAPTER 3

Negotiating Like a Pro

In the first two chapters of this book, I suggested which items are best to look for, and those items it's best to distance yourself from. The next step in becoming a successful Garage Sale Millionaire is learning the proper way to negotiate the best deals for your treasured finds.

The Art of the Deal

To master the art of the deal, you'll need to understand a few different techniques for becoming the greatest buyer you can be. Even though you won't become an expert negotiator overnight, the more you deal with items at garage sales, secondhand stores, estate auctions, storage unit auctions, and on eBay and Craigslist, the closer you'll come to achieving expert Garage Sale Millionaire status.

Being successful at negotiating is not based solely on how aggressive you are as a buyer. A more important skill is knowing how to talk someone down on their price to achieve the greatest deal possible. There are three main ways to buy an item: face-to-face, over the phone, or through the Internet. Of course, there are different tricks to employ for each of these methods that will yield the highest rate of success.

A very rare, 50-million-year-old fossil from Wyoming called
"Notogoneus/ Displomystus Aspiration." To obtain this
amazing item, I negotiated for two weeks and ended up
saving 41% off the original price!

Dealing with Someone Face to Face

When dealing with someone in person, the seller will be able to look at you in real time and make a lasting judgment regarding what your financial status might be.

This is accomplished largely in part by the way you're dressed. Whatever you intend to purchase, whether it is jewelry, art, cars, or pretty much anything else—a salesperson will always size you up by giving you the once-over. I'm not saying this practice is fair or that I agree with it, but it is a reality.

Million $ Tip

One way salespeople size you up as a potential customer is by what you're wearing... especially your jewelry and shoes. Always leave the expensive accessories at home. People usually forget to dumb down these two personal items, and they are a dead give-away that you have more money to spend. This means less leverage for you, the buyer, in any bargaining or negotiation.

I know what you're thinking: People don't look at, or even take the time to notice, these types of personal details. I can guarantee you this happens all the time! Attention to detail and close observation help us, as salespeople, to better understand our buyer—meaning YOU.

When you participate in any type of deal, be it at a garage sale or an antique shop, art gallery, or collectibles store, you will want to dress appropriately. Don't get all dressed up for the occasion. Don't wear an expensive watch, never wear big, gaudy rings, and always leave designer clothes and shoes at home. When you're shopping for an item that is going to require negotiation, you'll want to dress appropriately for the experience. Looking the part, especially in the way you're dressed, is one of the main considerations that will help you become a master negotiator and a successful Garage Sale Millionaire.

I like to wear something simple like a pair of jeans and a shirt. Button-down shirts are fine, and a pair of plain tennis shoes is also an option. The only acceptable piece of jewelry to wear would be a wedding ring. If you have a big diamond ring, leave it at home, and wear a simple gold band instead if you have one. An inexpensive or casual watch is also acceptable. When salespeople see that you can easily afford the finer things, it's much harder to negotiate any kind of bargain with them. Driving a high- end car is another dead giveaway that you are well off. If you don't have access to a clunker and you arrive at the store in your nice flashy vehicle, never park in front of the store where the salesperson can see what you're driving. Leave it down the street and walk a block.

As you walk around the store, always be cordial and pleasant. Never act aloof or rude towards the salesperson. As soon as you're deemed discourteous or difficult, your chances of getting a better deal go right out the window. Salespeople will always be more accommodating to a potential customer who is polite and affable. They will literally jump through hoops for you

When you find something you like, you don't have to pretend you didn't see the item or don't want the item to ask for a deal on it. You should always examine the piece closely and make sure it's something you have a strong desire to buy. If you need to leave the store to do your research and return later, this is always considered an acceptable practice.

Traveling back and forth to the store once or twice is fine, but if you start coming back three, four, or even five times to look at the same item, you will hurt your chances of making a good deal. In the best-case scenario, you'll want to leave only once, then come back and make the appropriate offer.

Enter a store, browse to your heart's content, find the items that interest you, make notes if necessary, and then perhaps go home for a while and do some research on your computer. Then, when you feel confident you are armed with all the knowledge you need to make an informed assessment, go back, and make your best offer.

If you're completely certain you want to make a purchase, take a good look at the item and confirm that it's in a condition to your liking.

Million $ Tip

The owner of a store will always make you the best deal. A store manager or gallery director will only make you an average deal. The reason store managers and gallery directors will not offer any type of deep discount is that the money you save on an item comes directly out of their pocket. I also guarantee that, in most stores, sales-people are on a commission only pay basis, and will not make you a deal on much of anything. If you have your sights set on a high dollar item and you want to get the best deal possible, you will need to get in contact with the owner of the business.

Ensure the item has not been restored and that it has all its original packaging. If the original packaging is not included, or it is damaged, you'll need to decide if this is something you really want to buy. I will discuss the importance of having original packaging, and how this directly affects resale value, in Chapter 7. If your item requires accessories (a set of keys, for example), you need to make certain that everything is included before negotiating a price.

When you're ready to make a purchase, ask if there is an owner available, so you can speak to someone in charge to start the negotiation process. When speaking to the owner, always be friendly and civil. Never be critical of the item you want to purchase; it's always amazing to me how many people will insult the very items they want to buy. What constitutes an insult? If the item is an antique, don't begin the conversation by stating that the item is heavily overpriced or in bad condition.

The person standing in front of you fully understands that, when you're trying to find the less attractive points relative to an item, you're really trying to position it at a lesser price. In simple words, this is a negotiation tool. Now, if you point out scratches or dents that are not so obvious, that is fantastic and considered fair game. When you do this, always acknowledge that the item in question is nonetheless a nice piece. Remember, never be too negative.

Begin your dialogue with the store owner by saying you're looking at a piece and that the item is of genuine interest to you. Also, take time to make the usual small talk. There's nothing wrong with asking how long the store owner has been in business or pointing out that it's unfortunate he or she has to work on the weekend or on such a nice day. By finding something in common, the owner will look at you more as a person than a client, and more as a friend than a mark. It's very important to have a good working relationship with the owner, or whoever is in charge, when you start the negotiation process on an item of interest to you. If you do this, there's a better-than-average chance he or she will like you, take an interest in you, and give you a much better deal.

Make sure you know the value of the item that you're negotiating. Check completed sales on eBay. It could be that the price the store is asking is way too high and not worth negotiating on, or you just found a great deal. The more information you have before you start the negotiation, the better.

Dealing with Someone over the Telephone or by Email

Now that you understand a few of the tricks used to negotiate a better deal when working with someone face-to-face, let's discuss how to handle other forms of negotiation. These types of transactions take place over the telephone or via email. Using methods other than the face-to-face approach is a bit trickier but, with some experience, they can be mastered. Because you're not dealing with someone face to face, you don't have to worry about your looks. You don't need to speak any differently than you normally would or put on airs to make your point. You will, however, need to pay extra careful attention to what is being said.

The average person relies heavily on using email and the internet to get the best deals on a broad range of merchandise. Before the current popularity of the Internet (and society's increasing dependence upon it), high-speed technology meant using the telephone to negotiate a deal. The phone is still a potent weapon in any Garage Sale Millionaire's arsenal, but the internet makes doing many things more efficient and easier.

Therefore, let's turn our focus to transacting business by email. Many businesses have items available for sale on the Internet. In antique stores, art galleries, and secondhand stores, there is usually a designated person who places items for sale on the company's website. A good website operated by a proficient company is updated regularly, with sold items removed and new items posted as soon as they become available. The Internet allows for business to not only take place locally, but on a national or international level as well. This makes it an important sales tool for stores.

If you find an item you're interested in buying on a website, the best thing to do is email the owner directly. In your message, identify and describe the item you are interested in (be sure to include the item number associated with the posting) and make it very clear—in a nice way, of course—that you have a limited budget. You are a serious buyer and want to purchase something right away, but you need the very best deal he or she is willing to offer. In your email, you need to emphasize that your decision to buy an item is all about price and that you are also looking somewhere else. When you discuss price with a store owner, you'll want to let them know right away that, if he or she wants your business, you will need to be offered their best price—immediately.

> **Million $ Tip**
>
> Always be aware that the negotiation of any item, or multiple items, is not a speed contest. Take your time and listen carefully to the other person as he or she negotiates their end of the deal so that you can get the best price possible.

Many shop owners, art gallery directors, and store managers prefer communicating by phone because they know they'll have one or two shots to get you to buy. Convincing you to buy is contingent upon these individuals making you the right (best) offer. If they are unsuccessful at getting you to make a purchase in their first or second call, there's a good chance you will have already obtained the item elsewhere. If you're contacting the seller from another state, you'll want to make your location known so you are recognized as exempt from sales tax. This will make the transaction a bit easier for the seller as well. Also, let the seller know you will accept the easiest, least expensive method for shipping the item. You do not want to incur costly overnight charges for shipping. Always inquire about getting insurance on your shipment to protect it while it's in transit.

Making any kind of deal over the Internet (i.e. email) is, in my opinion, the toughest way to negotiate. Why? There's no real sense of bonding between the seller and the customer, or vice versa. Many store owners don't feel as though they have a reason to give you a better deal, because they don't know you or anything about you.

> **Million $ Tip**
>
> When buying across state lines, tax free is not a guarantee anywhere—so ask!

If you're calling about an item you saw on the store's website, you will want to start a dialogue with the owner immediately. Find some sort of common ground, so that the seller will begin to feel comfortable with you. Once you've found your common ground, it's time to begin to negotiate.

The Basics of Negotiation

In this chapter, I have discussed the best way to work with people in person, as well as remotely through telephone or email. I've also made you aware of how sellers instantly size up buyers, and what they're thinking about during every aspect of the sales process. I've given you the essential information about what goes into a sale; now it is time to discuss how to properly negotiate a sale to get the best deal possible. If an item is rare, time is not on your side!

When you begin discussing an item you want to buy, you'll definitely want to ask questions specific to that item. Once again, always make sure the item you're interested in is the exact item you want to purchase. Ask everything you want to know about the item, even if you're positive it's the piece for you. Even if you're 100% certain you know everything there is to know, there's nothing wrong with asking the seller for more information. You never know what details might be divulged as you discuss the specifics of a particular item. Remember, nothing is final until you spend your hard-earned money—so why not try to find out as much information as possible?

After you've spoken for a few moments about the item you want to buy, it's time to mention the fact that, although you're really interested, you have a limited budget to spend. Let the seller know how much you like the item, but also that you don't know if you can afford the asking price. Now is the time to ask if something can be done to help you out on the price. The seller will probably begin to tell you that their price is very low already.

Some stores will offer you free layaway. A layaway

is basically a way of paying for items in installments. You put a small amount of money down on the item as a first payment and then continue to make small payments every month until the item is paid in full. Your purchase will remain in the store until all the layaway payments are made. A layaway payment plan simply makes it easier for you to pay for an item by allowing you to make smaller payments, spread across a set period, instead of having to pay in full all at once. Let the seller know you appreciate knowing about their layaway policy, and that you might eventually want to use this as a means of payment. By mentioning that you may accept some sort of layaway agreement to purchase the item, you could get an immediate break on the price.

Usually shop owners, gallery directors, and managers will decrease the price by up to 10%, knowing the item will soon be out of the store. Also, wait until the end of the month for deals from sellers. Store owners would rather take a percentage hit on the item to accelerate immediate cash flow and free up space in their store right away. Believe it or not, this is a common practice within the industry. But you're not looking for a meager 10% discount on items you have a serious interest in. You did not buy this book so you could find a way of getting a better deal that only amounts to 10% off.

Now you're going to say to the person you are negotiating with, "Thanks, but a 10% discount isn't such a great price for me. There's a store closer to where I live that will offer more than 10% off the exact item you have in your store.

However, I do prefer to conduct all my business out of state, so I don't have to pay any sales tax." By making this statement, you could receive an immediate price drop on the item you want to buy, but you will also help the seller better relate to you. This lets the person you're dealing with know that you will be a serious buyer in the future.

All sellers love to hear, "I'm starting my collection, and I need many more of these kinds of collectibles." They absolutely love finding out that they've come across someone new to work with, both now and in the future. This is the point where you say, "You know, right now we're at 10%, and I appreciate the discount, but I was thinking of a number closer to 30% off."

Million $ Tip

It is never a good deal if you cannot get the deal completed. This is one of the best tips I can ever give you regarding mastering the art of the deal. As a Garage Sale Millionaire, you are buying a particular item because you know there is a substantial profit awaiting you upon its resale. In the end, you may lose out on a large financial windfall from the resale of any item by asking for too deep of a discount and eventually losing the item.
You most certainly cannot make any money from the sale of an item that you do not actually own!

Now's the right moment to reference whatever discount you're comfortable with discussing and ask if you can have the item at the seller's maximum discount. If you ask for more than a 50% discount over the telephone, more than likely you're going to hear a dial tone very quickly. Furthermore, if you're asking for more than a 50% discount in person, you may get the cold shoulder and whoever you are dealing with may shut the door on future business dealings forever.

I recommend you go to a percentage somewhere

between 15% and 45%. You should realize that whatever final sales price you agree upon, the seller is going to offer a final sales price higher than your lowest proposal. If you try to get a discount between 40% and 45%, the seller will more than likely offer a discount that is half of your offer.

If you truly love the item and know it's a great find, be careful not to lose it, no matter what the final price may end up being. You should always be ready to concede the final price. I can't tell you how many times I wanted the best deal in the world and ended up losing out on the deal altogether because I wouldn't accept a final sales price of barely 5% over my final offer. A day or two later, I usually found that the item was sold to someone else. I could have made a huge profit from reselling the item but got greedy and blew the deal.

After you've agreed on a price, you should be willing to make your payment arrangements over the phone. There are two ways to proceed: You can offer to come in and pay cash for a better deal, or you can offer to pay with a credit card. If you don't live in the city or state where the business you're dealing with is located, then it's best to pay by credit card or PayPal. In this case, you also want to make sure the seller offers free shipping.

One of the benefits of negotiating over the phone is that, if you're still unhappy with the price, you have the option of leaving your name and number for a callback. Tell the person you are negotiating with, "If you're interested in the price I offered, please give me a call. I'm going to consider your offer for the next few days (or a week... whatever time frame you are comfortable using), and then I'll make up my mind". The reason you must give the seller a set number of days is that you don't want their cat-and-mouse game to continue for an indefinite amount of time. Your decisiveness and commitment to offering a set time limit will entice and motivate the seller to make the deal. There's a very good chance that, if the counter price you offered is fair, the seller will call you back to make the sale. If you're impatient (try not to be), if you need this piece as a gift, or if you're afraid of losing the item, then you need to make the deal right then and there on the phone.

If time is on your side and it's acceptable to lose out on the item, try to bluff the seller by proposing a very deep discount with the hope that he or she will call you back to accept your lowball offer. It never hurts to try a bluff with the owner, as long as you are prepared to lose out in the end. I have a 70% success rate when I bluff. Sometimes, the seller will call you back to apologize and tell you they won't be able to make the deal at the low price you offered. He or she may ask, again, if there is any way you might still want the item at a higher price than your final offer. Depending on what you really want to spend, you can discuss another final price and see if the seller is intent on working with you to move the item out of their store and into your possession.

Expert Negotiating Strategies

I would love to give you a detailed look at and talk you through the negotiation process, based on my decades of personal and professional experience. I've worked in the art field for about 40 years. I've also been an art and memorabilia collector for most of my life. The following example perfectly illustrates what the negotiation process is all about. Let's take an item originally marked $500 and negotiate this item down to something more affordable!

You'll want to start by offering the seller a little more than half of the original sale price. That means a little less than a 50% discount. If you go under $250, you'll basically insult the seller. This is not a very good strategy to use, but if you have no problem losing your chances of getting a good deal, you can always try it. Remember our bluff example earlier in this chapter. Of course, if you're serious about acquiring the item, I strongly recommend against this strategy. When people offer me less than half the price of any item I'm selling, I am personally insulted. I never priced items in my own gallery too high, but at a fair price where I can make an honest living.

So, be forewarned, if you were to use that tactic on me, maybe one time in 50 would I bite and make the deal. If it's worth it to you to try to get the best deal in the world and you believe this sort of tactic works, then, by all means, give it your best shot. Don't be surprised when you're asked to leave stores if you choose to employ this tactic. When you really like the store, shop, or gallery and want to come back in the future, the goal is not to insult people. Remember, sellers need to earn a living as well!

I recommend offering a little bit above half of the original sales price, perhaps using $275 to $300 as an appropriate starting point, based on the $500 price tag of our example. The seller will always counter higher; he or she will never say okay to your first offer. So, whatever you do, you don't want to give your best dollar offer knowing the counteroffer will be much higher. You could start by offering $450, which is quite high for a first offer, but I guarantee the counteroffer will come back at $475. By starting your negotiations with the salesperson with a lower initial offer, you'll leave room for both of you to meet in the middle, and eventually come to an acceptable final sale price.

For fun, let's go bare bones and offer a very low starting price of $275. (This first offer is to buy the item at a 45% discount. Good for you!) The seller will probably counter your offer at $400. Pay careful attention here. At this point during the negotiation, you will want to be holding the item in your hands, if it's not too large…an old clock, an antique or collectible toy, a coin, a vase, etc. This action shows the seller a seemingly sincere and emotional attachment to the item; you are actually sending a signal that you have marked the item as your own, and you are making a statement by literally holding onto it. Now, as you stand with the item in your hands, having offered $275, the seller counteroffers $425. This is $25 more than you expected the counteroffer to be. If the seller does this, look him straight in the eye, then glance at the item in your hands and shake your head back and forth. Put on your best sad face and place the item back on the shelf.

You may not think this is going to accomplish anything, but right there the seller just got scared! He or she may have felt a little twinge or a funny feeling, thinking they just lost you as a customer. It also just occurred to them that their commission on the item you were holding is about to leave the store, right along with you. While placing the item back where you found it, you should be shaking your head and muttering under your breath, in a very disheartened tone, "Yeah, that price is more than I can spend…it's too much." At this moment, it's almost a guarantee that the person who was assisting you is going to come after you, magically dropping their price. Let the tried-and-true psychological maneuver known as "the put back" work for you.

Let's go back to the seller's $425 counteroffer. Usually, after an initial counteroffer of $425 is made, the next best counteroffer will be somewhere near $375. When you make your counter to their counteroffer, come up a little bit in your new price, but do not touch the item again. Never touch the item until you both are a little closer to agreeing on a final sales price. If the seller offers $375 (and the seller usually will), you counter the offer with $325. The goal will be to stand pat at $325, which is a 35% discount from the original $500 price!

If you are sure the seller is not going to budge any lower than the $375 he or she offers you, then you have two options: The first is holding firm at $325, saying, "I'm sorry, but I just can't accept that price. Thanks anyway for your time." Always wish the seller a good day and then leave the store. There's a very good chance this will rattle the seller's cage and he or she may agree to your $325 price. I must tell you that this strategy works like a charm for me seven out of ten times.

Now, if this course of action hasn't worked for you and you get to the door without making the deal, you may want to turn around and nicely say, "Is it okay to leave my name and telephone number with you? If you change your mind on my offer, and I hope you do, please call me right away." At this point in the negotiation process, write down your name and telephone number and leave the information with the proprietor. Another option is to counteroffer once again with a final price of $350. This final price is $25 more than your $325 offer, but still $25 below the top counteroffer of $375. Tell the seller you will take it at $350, and that is the best you can do. There is still a good chance the seller will accept your final offer because it is so close to the middle point.

There is always a middle point in all negotiations, and usually, people will accept the middle ground. The seller might hem and haw a bit, but he or she will usually accept.

This is the best example I can give to you, my future Garage Sale Millionaire, to show you how proper negotiation is performed in any situation, in any sales venue. This kind of negotiation should be employed at art galleries, garage sales, antique shops, collectibles stores, or any place where a customer, salesperson, and merchandise is involved. I have had a 70% success rate with this negotiation strategy, and I've made some good money over the years by implementing these tactics.

As a former art gallery owner, if I'm given contact information during the negotiation process, I will start thinking about accepting the highest price the customer has offered. Then I find myself thinking, "Well, maybe the price the customer offered was not too bad and the offer was not all that low." If I've had a week when sales were a little lower than expected and I don't have anyone else interested in the piece, I'll call every one of my customers to see who might be interested. If I still don't have any takers after making all my calls, there's a good chance I will call back the customer who made me an offer and accept it.

Another negotiating strategy that works to save you an extra 2% to 4% on items is offering to pay with cash. Now that you have the item you want at a price you can live with, it's time to inform the seller you'll be paying by credit card. The seller will say, "Okay," because you already know the seller takes credit cards, just not American Express. (Remember what I said in Chapter 1: American Express charges the seller a higher per-transaction percentage than all the other credit card companies: 2.8-

4%.) Once the seller accepts the idea that you'll be paying by credit card, you have one final card to play to get an additional 2%-4% off the sale price of the item. After you make it known you will be paying by credit card, simply ask, "I can use my credit card, but I also have cash. If I pay with cash, would you be willing to take off another 3%?"

> **Million $ Tip**
>
> When using a credit card, make sure to pay with a card that gives you cash back for your purchases. Several cards offer up to 2% cash back.

Not many sellers will say no to that. Why? The first and most important reason is that they're going to have to pay the credit card companies for processing each credit card transaction. If the merchant accepts cold, hard cash, there will be no additional processing fees.

> **Million $ Tip**
>
> Never send checks or money orders in the mail. Don't wire money if you haven't previously worked with the seller. Once you send money with any of the aforementioned methods, you have no recourse if events go poorly and there is a dispute with your transaction. A good strategy is to use PayPal Goods & Services and/or a credit card which both allow you to dispute transactions if they turn out to be fraudulent.

Secondly, when you pay with a credit card, the merchant doesn't receive payment at the time the transaction takes place. On average, it takes two to three days to have the money from a credit card sale deposited into the seller's bank account by the respective credit card company. So, with every deal, you will want to have cash as a back-up whenever possible. Cash will always leverage the deal. When you agree on a price, always ask for 3% less than the final sale price if you pay for the item entirely in cash. If the store owner offers only 2%, you should immediately counter with, "No, then it's not worth it."

Once you've secured your discount, consider whether or not you'd like to purchase a second piece from the store. Perhaps it could be another chair, or a decorative vase, to place alongside your antique dining room table. Be sure to ask the seller what discount he or she can offer if you purchase two, or even three pieces.

This is where your discount can grow exponentially. Never put all your cards on the table by telling the seller you want to buy more than one piece at the beginning of your negotiation. If you do, you will lose the leverage you had. The key to negotiating this way is to bring the seller into your negotiations at a very gradual pace, and at a time when you have the optimal vantage point. Start to reel in the seller with the initial thought that you are only going to buy one item.

Once you agree on a price for that one item, drop the hammer and let the seller know you are actually thinking about two or three additional pieces. The seller should instantly give you the original discount, plus maybe a little bit more. You want the best deal possible and, from my experience, you're more than likely to get it!

Once your offer has been accepted, you've paid for your purchase in cash, and the item is all wrapped up and ready to go, make sure the seller has your complete contact information. By having your name, telephone number, and email address on file, store personnel can call you if anything interesting arrives that may be on your wish list or could perhaps pique your interest. You've also made an informal announcement to the store that you want to continue to do business with them.

As a result of your actions, you've made a valuable ally who will go to battle for you in the collectibles business and give you a heads-up regarding the great finds that come through their vast information pipeline. Store personnel will search for new items for you. They'll be available to answer any questions you may have about items that may be of special interest to you, and they'll be happy to do so. Additionally, now you will have someone to share announcements and provide expert recommendations concerning expos, events, and gatherings you should attend to further your knowledge. By establishing an ongoing relationship with an established collectibles business, you'll be privy to any future store sales, or VIP/invite-only events. Over time, if you continue to spend more money with them, you will get even better deals on items you want to buy in the future.

Million $ Tip

Don't forget to use your resources! eBay now allows you to scan barcodes on books and will pull up exact matches so you can see the current pricing on the item. You can also search by picture on eBay just like you can on Google, but it will only search through eBay's exact match results. By using resources like this, as well as books, articles, etc. you will be the best negotiator in no time!

Are You a Garage Sale Millionaire?

Mastering the art of the deal takes a little practice, but if you follow my personal strategies outlined in this chapter, you should move to the head of the class very quickly. Any successful Garage Sale Millionaire will eventually master, and be consistently proficient in, the art of the deal. Remember:

- Take your time
- Be knowledgeable
- Understand the process
- Remember to have fun
- Be cordial and respectful,
- Know that by implementing what you've learned in this chapter, you're going to have a better opportunity to purchase the item you want at the price you want.

By following these few simple steps, you'll master the art of the deal in no time! Good luck!

CH4PTER

Fakes, Replicas, and Restorations
How Not to Get "Taken"

For every collectible, there exists a fake or replica made of that same item. If you have a collectible you love and it's worth money, someone, somewhere, has already realized they can make more money off it by creating an authentic-looking fake. Whether the item is an autographed piece of sports memorabilia, a Civil War-era item, a piece of American presidential ephemera, a signed movie poster, or a 125-year-old antique—there's always someone working diligently to replicate that item so they can make a quick buck off you. That, dear reader, is a guarantee.

When you finish reading this chapter, you'll have a thorough understanding of how to keep one step ahead of the people who create the frauds, fakes, and restorations—so that when you place your hard-earned money down, you won't be ripped off. Acquiring as much information as possible about the collecting process will help you protect yourself from being taken by these nefarious individuals. In the following pages, I will personally share the secret tips that have protected me through my 30-plus years of collecting.

How to ProtectYourself

With all the rules, regulations, and laws our society has in place, how can people continue to blatantly produce products that mimic authentic items? More importantly, how in the world can these individuals make such consistently good money, and evade the law, time after time? I know the idea may come as a shock to you, but this type of fraud is commonplace. It is one of the main reasons why I decided to write *The Garage Sale Millionaire*. I want to show you how to protect yourself from unscrupulous individuals and provide you with the knowledge that will prevent you from becoming another rip-off statistic.

Creating and passing off fakes, replicas, and restorations was far more difficult to accomplish in the past when people dealt with others in a more personal, one-on-one manner. Since the emergence of eBay, Craigslist, email, and the internet, this type of criminal activity has become increasingly easy to pull off. Moreover, an item manufactured today can be duplicated.

My goal here is to discuss which collectibles are the most lucrative and most often replicated by crooks, as well as where you are most likely to encounter fraudulent documentation, fakes, and replicas.

Protecting yourself against fraud, like many other processes detailed in this book, is easy enough to accomplish. All it takes is understanding some basic information and then implementing your new-found knowledge. After that, you can safely proceed with your Garage Sale Millionaire activities confident that you won't get cheated. In 1537, Francis Bacon said "Knowledge is Power," but today, it's what you do with your knowledge that holds power. Chapter 4 is all about helping you gain an understanding and awareness of fakes, replicas, and restorations so that you don't get cheated.

Presidential Memorabilia

Collecting presidential memorabilia is one of the most problematic areas collectors encounter. Why? As far back as 1789, when President George Washington was in office, certain individuals were authorized to sign the president's name for him.

Yes, you read that correctly. Often, a signature from a president is actually signed by a secretary, another staff member, or even a friend or family member, rather than the president himself. If the

Million $ Tip

Presidential autographs are very valuable and are among some of the most often forged collectibles.

signature you have on your document was not signed directly by a particular president, the value of the item decreases by 75% or more. Oth- er items used by presidents—such as clothes, blotters, or even dentures—are also highly collectible, but these items must have a verified certificate and/or auction record from where and when the item last sold.

Unless you're an expert in the art of collecting signed presidential memorabilia, it's very difficult to determine which signatures are authentic and which are not. This is one collectible you don't want to gamble on because even the experts tend to get fooled. You need to be very careful when buying authentic signed historical documents, especially when it involves presidential signatures.

Sports and Entertainment Memorabilia

People are buying and selling fake autographs 24/7. The only way you can fully protect yourself against fraud is to verify the authenticity or source of the autograph. It's a known fact that for every actor, director, and professional athlete who lends their signature to an item, there are probably two signatures from the same celebrity verified as fakes. The Emmy award- winning CBS News program *60 Minutes* once broadcast a segment about the potential pitfalls of collecting signed sports memorabilia. After speaking with numerous experts in the field of collecting, *60 Minutes* concluded that roughly half of all signatures on the market are fakes.

Million $Tip

If you want to make money dealing in the buying and selling of signatures, you'd better know your signatures. Astronauts, movie stars, entertainment moguls, presidents, athletes, business leaders— anyone who is or was famous, as well as infamous, may very likely have had a secretary or assistant signing for them.

Many people selling autographs will claim that they were actually present with the person who signed an item and personally witnessed the person attaching his or her signature to that item. One of my very good friends, a well-known professional in the autograph and collectibles business, has always said, "It doesn't matter how good the seller's story is if the buyer can't personally back it up." Basically, he means that, if the signature is not real, then whatever story is being told to prove the authenticity of that autograph doesn't even remotely matter.

It's astonishing to me (and keep in mind that I am actually in the art and collectibles business) how many times over the years I've heard similar stories, from almost every autograph seller. They proudly say, "I was there and watched (fill in a famous person's name) sign it." Then, I'll take that signature to the back room of my gallery and compare the seller's so-called original to a signature I know to be verifiably authentic. I almost always find that their so-called original is not even close to being a match.

Only when I advise the seller that their signature isn't authentic, do they admit, "We didn't watch them sign it. A secretary took the paper to another room, came back, and handed it to us."

Regardless of the story coming from the seller, you want to have a Certificate of Authenticity, or COA, to accompany any item you might want to purchase. As I mentioned in Chapter 2, a COA is a document the seller issues which guarantees the purchased item is authentic. Of course, a COA can always be faked by a seller, and many people will tell you a COA is not worth the paper it's printed on. Almost anyone can print out a COA.

> **Million $ Tip**
>
> Watch out if you bid at charitable auctions. If you see a good deal on a signature, it could be fake. In my experience, there's a good chance that music and movie memorabilia lots could wind up being fake, too.

It's as easy as printing out a generic certificate, which can be generated with any number of inexpensive desktop publishing software programs.

To make sure your COA will be recognized as representing an authentic item, always do business with a reputable art and collectibles dealer and always ask for a money-back guarantee on the item you want to buy. Signatures from individuals in the entertainment industry, both in film and television, are usually acquired at public events, on the set, through private meetings, or from individuals and autograph companies who have access to these types of celebrities. Page signatures are obtained when stores or agents contract with an athlete or celebrity to autograph multiple memorabilia pieces, in exchange for a set fee. This type of arrangement usually occurs with sports figures, movie stars, former presidents, or anyone whose signature has an assigned value.

When this is the case, there should be a contract for you to examine, as well as actual photos of the celebrity signing the items. If you're shopping at a reputable establishment, there's a good chance that the signature is legitimate. Stores such as The Upper Deck, Mounted Memories, and Latitude Sports Marketing, as well as many other memorabilia businesses, contract these types of signings many times throughout the year.

Million $ Tip

If you're serious about getting into the business of buying and selling autographs, you should buy *Collecting Autographs and Manuscripts* by Charles Hamilton. Because this is such a diverse topic, you can never learn enough on the subject.

However, if the COA states only the location where the signing took place without an address, phone number, or working website, then the COA is most likely junk, and you should steer clear. When collectible merchandise and memorabilia are professionally graded, the agency verifying an item's authenticity will affix a sticker that displays a one-of-a-kind image in the form of a hologram, proving the item is deemed to be authentic. Before you buy an item with a verified-as-authentic signature, you should always know what the signature you're attempting to collect really looks like. There are many resources available to the autograph and memorabilia collector that include photographs so you can look and compare what may be authentic to what is authentic.

One fantastic company for self-verifying and self-authenticating celebrity signatures, in both the sports and entertainment industries, is **Star Tiger** (www.startiger.com). As of 2024, StarTiger.com has an exhaustive database of over 1,100,000 scanned celebrity autographs, 430,000+ celebrities listed in their database (with addresses and contact information), and over 1,200,000 forum posts from members. There are multiple scans and examples of almost every signature listed on the website, so you can compare the variations in a celebrity's personal signature from item to item. Full access to the website does require a membership fee, but you can perform basic searches free of charge.

Million $ Tip

To gain an advantage on your Garage Sale Millionaire journey, proactively search out and make friends with your local antique dealers. Not only will these individuals help advise you about the antique business, but they will also make you great deals when they know you are in the business of buying and selling antiques.

Antiques

There are companies located in every part of the world whose sole purpose is to replicate antiques. What do I mean by replicate? This type of antique furniture is built from newly sourced, raw materials, and then roughed up, distressed, and placed in the weather to fade or rust. These manufacturing companies will try anything they can to make their product look old and worn. To the untrained eye, these newly made antiques look convincingly authentic. Of course, the result of this unscrupulous business practice is that those good people often wind up paying for fraudulent products.

Fortunately, most conscientious shops know the difference between a genuine antique and a replica. There are, however, less-than-honest dealers that not only won't tell you the difference but will charge you as if the item were an authentic antique. They will even go as far as to say it is an antique! But the good news is that there are ways you can look at a piece to determine if what you're seeing is genuine.

The first thing you need to do is to flip the item over and look at its underside. If the piece you're looking at is a table, get down on your hands and knees and examine the underside of the table. Look at the way the item is put together. Were any screws used? How about nails? What specific kinds of screws and nails were used? Certain types of nails indicate an item is newly manufactured. For example, if you see the flathead nails used today in furniture manufacturing, it's a dead giveaway that you're looking at a newly made item. In fact, nails used to build furniture over 100 years ago were very long, skinny, and sort of lumpy, and their heads were not perfectly round, since blacksmiths of the era made every single nail by hand. If glue or staples were used on the piece you're inspecting, you need to stay away—you are most likely looking at a restoration or a fake. Many collectors disagree on whether the cleaning and restoration of an antique item is an acceptable practice and, many times, antiques are restored incorrectly. When done properly, restorations can be per- formed without damaging the item; the process will usually bring the piece back to its original state. I will cover restored antiques in more detail later on in this chapter.

The easiest way to find out if there is any glue on an item, or to verify that a restoration was done properly, is to use a black light. Whether the item is furniture or pottery, if glue has been used in the restoration process, it will visibly stand out when held under the black light; it will fluoresce, or glow. What makes these added glue marks so obvious are the chemical compounds used in making the glue.

If possible, take the object into a room where you can control the lighting. While the room is darkened, turn on your black light and carefully inspect the item in question. Certain colors and pigments, such as those found in glue compounds, absorb the invisible light and then discharge that light. When this discharge occurs, a glowing effect can be observed.

Million $Tip

A black light will determine if a piece of art has been restored and can even identify a missing signature. What do I mean by a missing signature? When a piece of art was originally created, the artist may never have placed their signature on that particular piece. A black light will confirm whether a signature was added after the fact by a collector. If this is the case, then the piece you coveted for its resale potential loses almost all its value.

Hopefully, you won't encounter any tell-tale traces of glue, and nothing else you observe will have any glowing properties. Black lights are extremely helpful in determining if an item has been improperly restored or if it truly is a genuine antique. The difference between an improperly restored item and an unrestored antique item is big money.

Jewelry

When purchasing jewelry, I want to strongly warn you that diamond counterfeiting is a big business. When someone is trying to sell a fake diamond, they will more than likely present you with a counterfeit grading report too, to support their claim that the diamond is verifiably authentic.

To make matters worse, even authentic diamonds are not always thoroughly and carefully examined during the grading process. What exactly do I mean by this? If a jeweler personally examined and graded the diamond or stone, he or she could be off; they might misjudge the diamond by several different grades or colors. Such discrepancies directly affect the value of the jewel and its retail price. To protect yourself, you'll always want to have a diamond graded by the **Gemological Institute of America (GIA)** (www.gia.edu). The diamond grading criteria set by the GIA is the preferred, nationally accepted standard. Here is a quote taken directly from the GIA website: "Because diamonds are so valuable, it is essential to have a universal grading system for comparing their quality. In the 1940s and 1950s, GIA developed the 4Cs and the GIA International Diamond Grading System to objectively compare and evaluate diamonds."

Million $Tip

14 karat gold is only 58.33% gold; 18 karat gold is 75% gold; 24 karat gold is pure gold. If a piece of jewelry is gold, a stamp will appear somewhere on the item noting its purity. However, just because an item is stamped 10K, 14K, or 18K doesn't mean it is real gold. Some fraudulent companies will stamp gold-plated items as real. The same goes for silver items.

The 4Cs include:

- **Carat**—Diamonds and other gemstones are weighed and categorized in metric carats. One metric carat is equal to 0.2 grams.

- **Color**—Diamonds are valued by how closely they approach colorlessness. The less color a diamond has, the higher its value.

- **Clarity**—Diamonds without faults, inclusions, or blemishes are rare. Of course, the rarer a diamond, the higher it will be valued. Diamonds are assigned a clarity grade which ranges from Flawless (FL) on the top end of the grade range, to Obvious Inclusions (I3) on the lowest end of the grade range.

- **Cut**—Cut measures the verifiable level of craftsmanship applied in cutting the symmetry, shape, proportions and polish into a stone. The better the cut of a diamond, the higher its value.

This grading methodology also applies to gold. Just because gold is stamped 14K or 18K does not mean the carat grading is correct. If you buy gold or silver outside of the United States, even if it's marked with an authentic-looking stamp, chances are good you're not purchasing the real thing. If you don't trust your seller—buyer beware!

Always know your grader and always make sure any pieces of jewelry you purchase are certified by a respected organization, the same way GIA is respected throughout the gemological industry.

Additionally, make sure you receive a money-back guarantee, and always use your credit card to purchase jewelry. By using a credit card, you will have the most recourse regarding any transaction, just in case you need to exchange or return an item for a refund. Jewelry is one area of collecting where many people get taken because they don't realize they've been duped until it's too late. Again, when buying jewelry, remember to be extremely careful.

Restorations and Replicas... Not as Advertised!

I haven't had a lot of good things to say about restorations in this chapter. In most cases, restoring an item will significantly reduce its value, because restoration compromises originality. When people purchase antiques, they want to see original finishes, colors, stains, hardware—even screws and nails. Once an item is upgraded, it will no longer be an antique, but a hybrid between old and new. But believe it or not, restorations are not all bad. If you know you're buying something that has been restored, and the item is exactly what you want at a price point you find reasonable, then good for you! By all means, enjoy your purchase.

When I speak badly about restorations, I'm referring to the practice from the viewpoint of a Garage Sale Millionaire. I can't tell you how many times I've talked to individuals from across the United States who have been taken—they bought from a dealer selling what they thought to be an authentic antique, only to discover later that they've actually purchased a newly manufactured replica or a poorly completed restoration.

As I stated at the beginning of this chapter, "For every collectible, there exists a fake or replica made of that same item. If you have a collectible you love, and it's worth money, someone, somewhere, has already realized they can make more money off it by creating an authentic-looking fake." As a savvy Garage Sale Millionaire, you always need to be aware of this duplicitous practice. At any time, you could be misled into buying something that is not as advertised. Not only do you need to be aware of the possibility of restoration, but you must also be aware of how particular items are restored in practice. If the restoration is completed incorrectly, it can hurt the value of a piece.

Consider comic books, for instance. There are so many comic books available today in poor to extremely poor condition, in need of proper restoration. If you are a comic book collector and have an extensive collection, chances are good that one or two of your treasures have been restored at some time in the past. Comic book restorations are not entirely bad. A good restoration will be indistinguishable from an original. A restoration, when rendered properly, will decrease the value of your comic a little bit, but the subsequent value of your comic may be improved more than had it not been restored in the first place. It's only when the restoration is completed improperly that a comic book's value is diminished irreparably. Typically, restoration efforts will be focused on the front and back covers of the book. Check the inside cover pages for evidence of treatment, such as changes in sheen or texture, or fluorescence under a black light.

The restoration of antiques and comic books is

acceptable, but cleaning coins is not—period! If you clean coins, even just slightly, you will wear away the surface metal and cause very fine scratch marks. These scratch marks degrade the coin's overall quality, inevitably lowering the collectible value of the coin. Because of this, I never recommend cleaning coins. In my professional opinion, you will always do more harm than good.

There is a whole contingency of learned collectors and individuals who will argue both sides of this "to clean or not to clean" debate but, once again, you will probably want to leave your coins alone. By letting coins sit in their current state, even if they are a little rough and a bit dirty, you will always retain the value of the coin and avoid permanent damage.

Million $ Tip

Always get a money-back guarantee in writing. If this guarantee is listed in an auction on eBay, you should still print out a copy of the auction page, with the money-back guarantee, for your records. This paper trail will help you prove your case if you need to contact eBay's security department over a dispute with a seller.

If a Deal Sounds Too Good to Be True, It Probably Is

Whether you're looking to buy an item on eBay or Craigslist, at a thrift store, or in a secondhand store, you'll need to do more investigation prior to making any purchase. As the saying goes, "If a deal sounds too good to be true, it probably is."

On eBay, you must ask detailed questions. Request specifics about the seller's return policy, ask for better pictures, and always pay by credit card.

Remember, using a credit card gives you better recourse if your purchase is not as represented by the seller. With eBay it's a huge plus when the seller agrees to refund your money if you're not completely satisfied. Learn to live by these words on eBay: money-back guarantee. Typically, you'll only have a seven-day window to return an item, which is the norm on eBay. If you go beyond the seven days, the seller will most likely not honor your merchandise return, and you will be left with something you really don't want because you didn't keep better track of time.

Items obtained through Craigslist are handled in much the same way as items acquired on eBay, albeit with some minor differences. If you're buying an item from someone on Craigslist who's not in your area, implement the same strategies you do on eBay to verify the items. Ask detailed questions, ask for better pictures, ask about the seller's return policy, and always pay by credit card (usually through PayPal). As far as I know, there is rarely a seven-day return policy, or any return policy for that matter, for sales transacted on Craigslist, because much of the buying and selling is completed in person, or face-to-face, and almost every transaction is completed with cash. This is similar to the way sales are transacted at garage sales, which I discuss in detail in chapters 5 and 8. When you buy an item from someone locally on Craigslist, the transaction typically goes like this: People meet at a designated location, the item is presented to the buyer to determine if it is worth buying, money is exchanged, and both parties go their separate ways.

In secondhand stores and thrift stores, once you leave the premises you own the item you just purchased. When you buy something and walk out the door, you immediately become the official owner of that item. In these stores, the owner is counting on you to know what you're buying. If fakes are sold or items misrepresented in an antique store, the owner will usually return your money. The proprietors of antique stores don't want the bad publicity generated by doing something unethical or, in a worst-case scenario, illegal. Once again, for your financial protection, always pay with a credit card if something worries you about the item's authenticity. The best way to handle situations like this is not to purchase until you have done your research.

A Penny Saved

The most important takeaway of this chapter, and the point I most want to emphasize, is this: not everyone who sells memorabilia, antiques, or collectibles is honest. On another level, there are a few people in the business who genuinely do not know exactly what they have to sell, or do not know the true worth of their items when they place them in their stores, garage sales, or estate sales. However, there is a third group of people selling collectibles who prove to be very honest sellers who represent their items as verifiably authentic or properly label their replicas and reproductions. When you shop with the last type of individual listed here, you can comfortably complete your transaction with the confidence that you know exactly what you're buying.

Unfortunately, it's always up to you to be in a heightened state of awareness regarding everything you purchase. You always need to make sure that what you think you are buying, and what you're actually buying, is exactly the same thing. If you make a hasty decision—if you don't do the proper research to verify and authenticate an item, there is a very good chance you may buy something that has very little value, or no value whatsoever. The usual buyer beware adage applies, as always!

Million $ Tip

If an item comes with a Certificate of Authenticity, and you do not recognize the person authenticating it, it is best to Google who the authenticator is. There are some authenticators out there who are part of the forging process. If an item comes with a COA, it unfortunately does not guarantee that the item is legitimate.

When Ben Franklin said "A penny saved is a penny earned," he very well could have been referring to future Garage Sale Millionaires. As Garage Sale Millionaires, we fervently strive not to get "taken," because we know the subtle and not-so-subtle differences between what is truly authentic and what is fraudulent. We cut through the purposeful lies of unethical and unscrupulous shopkeepers and always complete the necessary research before even thinking about putting down our hard-earned money to purchase an item. By avoiding illegitimate or inauthentic items, we save our collective pennies and then use that money to purchase those hidden gems and buried treasures that will make us money in the future.

Remember that, at all times, you must be aware, be ready, and have all your bases covered! We are informed Garage Sale Millionaires, and we will not get taken by those individuals trying to sell us fakes.

A thought-to-be prized item: an original Aladdin magazine signed by
Robin Williams.

★BECKETT.

Date: July 20, 2023

Invoice #: 636400

To Whom It May Concern:

On behalf of Beckett Authentication, we regret to report that one or more of your recently submitted autographs for encapsulation, in our opinion, is not authentic. Each item has been marked with a label stating "Not Authentic – Did Not Pass Authentication" which means one or more of the following inconsistencies was present and prevented the item(s) from being certified:

- The signature has an atypical letter slant, angle, and pitch
- The formation of the letters and overlapping of strokes is irregular or unusual
- There is irregular spacing between the letters and/or names
- The signature lacks flow, rhythm, conviction, and spontaneity
- There are baseline issues, including misalignment and undulation
- The signature has been drawn slowly
- The signature exhibits excessive pen pressure and/or improper shading
- _____

On behalf of the Beckett Authentication Experts,

Steve Grad | Brian Sobrero | Charlie Price | Larry Studebaker

2700 Summit Ave, Suite 100
Plano, TX 75074

beckett-authentication.com
authentication@beckett.com

A letter from Beckett Authentication Services stating that the signature from Robin Williams is in fact not authentic, rendering the Aladdin magazine practically worthless.

CHAPTER 5

Launching Your Own Treasure Hunt

Now, it's time to launch your own great treasure-hunting adventure. In this chapter, you'll learn where to find those hidden gems, one-of-a-kind pieces, and extremely valuable treasures. Take your chance at attaining fame and fortune by becoming the next Indiana Jones of urban tombs. Your adventures will lead you to Goodwill stores, Salvation Army thrift stores, estate sales, second-hand stores, antique stores, auctions, storage units, and the online marketplace. So, without further ado, let's get started!

Tools of the Trade

Before you begin your quest for treasure-hunting immortality, you'll need some specific tools to ensure you have the best chance at success. By supplying yourself with the proper treasure-hunting tools from the start, you will be giving yourself the best opportunity to achieve financial success in your treasure-hunting activities.

Acquiring the right tools for your treasure-hunting adventures is simple. Let me start with a list of what you will need to venture off and make those great finds:

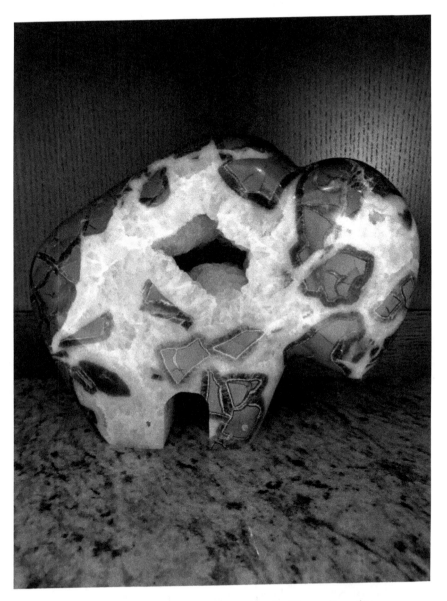

This is a fun item that I bought on Goodwill's auction site.
The retail value is somewhere between $350 and $450 on
eBay, and I bought it for $10 plus shipping.

- A fanny pack
- A good magnifying glass (with at least 10x magnification or higher)
- Sturdy work gloves
- White cotton gloves
- A pen
- A small notepad
- A large, high-powered flashlight
- Selfie Stick
- Smartphone or tablet
- Padlock (combination or keyed)
- Blacklight flashlight
- A box cutter or sturdy knife
- Magnet

Along with these tools, there are two more that could really help you out a lot in certain situations. The following treasure-hunting tools go above and beyond the scope of basic items listed above but are very beneficial to have.

A trailer, or any vehicle large enough to carry big loads—Having a large vehicle available is a huge asset, especially when you're looking to bid on the contents of a storage unit. I will cover storage units a little later in the chapter, when you buy the contents of a storage unit, you will usually need to move all the items within 24 hours after the purchase. Having a means of moving all those potential treasures without having to rent a truck will add to your efficiency and ability to get great deals. Whether it is a storage unit or an estate sale, a pickup truck or large work van will be helpful.

Sales tax license—A sales tax license could save you thousands of dollars over time. A sales tax license allows you to avoid directly paying tax on items you've acquired from estate sales, auctions, and storage unit sales since you'll be charging sales tax upon resale of your items. In most states, sales tax ranges from 6% to 14%, so for every $1,000 you spend, your savings will range from $60 to $140. This amount can add up substantially throughout the course of a year.

Additionally, if you sell the items you buy in your own state, you must charge sales tax. Currently, if you sell your items across state lines, you're not required to charge sales tax, but that is changing in some states. Of course, there are different tax zones for every city and county, so seek your accountant's advice on what to charge. A sales tax license will usually cost you approximately $10 to $100. These two additional treasure-hunting tools will streamline your business activities and, in the end, save you time and money. Now that you have all the necessary tools at your disposal, it's time to start hunting for goodies.

> **Million $ Tip**
>
> As a buyer, if you have a sales tax license or you are buying over state lines, you don't have to pay sales tax. Always check with your accountant, as rules may vary from state-to-state.

Where to Treasure Hunt

Always be alert! You never know when you might come across a buried treasure that could make you a substantial profit.

Secondhand Stores

When I talk about secondhand stores, I'm referring to places such as Salvation Army thrift stores, Goodwill Industry stores, AMVETS (American Veterans Thrift Stores), and consignment stores. These are all excellent locations to find some very valuable items.

People often ask me, "How can there possibly be treasure at secondhand stores?" Believe me when I tell you that people are making huge finds at these locations every day. In February 2009, a person found a piece of art at a secondhand store that was verified to be 150 years old. An appraiser friend of mine valued it and, wouldn't you know, that buried treasure was eventually auctioned at **Sotheby's** (www.sothebys.com) for $450,000! That treasure was found at a Goodwill Industry store. The item was waiting in the store for what could have been days to weeks to months. One day, because someone knew what to look for, they found a treasure worth close to half a million dollars. It's an amazing story—and it's true!

Whether you're cleaning up your home or someone else's, you're bound to find items that could eventually be worth a lot of money. Opportunities lie in wait in places you might never imagine. Perhaps a family friend might need help cleaning out their attic or garage, or in an unfortunate but almost inevitable situation, a family member may pass away, and you could find yourself with items that are no longer needed.

Million $ Tip

If you are close to a resort town, you will definitely want to visit their second-hand stores. You are guaranteed to find some wonderful and amazing things that were donated by the local residents.

After everything is gathered and cleaned, people usually just load their found items in a truck and try to help their community by taking everything to a local thrift store. By choosing this easy way out as your first option—and not taking into consideration the money that could be made from what you collected—you've made a huge mistake. This is how items, like the previously mentioned 150-year-old piece of art, get discarded. *It happens every day in second-hand stores.*

I recommend you go to secondhand stores weekly, usually at the beginning of the week. I find Mondays or Tuesdays are the best days to visit and do your treasure hunting. These are the days of the week when shelves are completely restocked with new merchandise. Stores receive most of their goods over the weekend and the employees work very hard to price everything for placement on their shelves early in the week. If you really want to be thorough and persistent, check back more often. The more you visit these businesses, the better chance you have of finding that item worth hundreds, even thousands, of dollars.

Secondhand stores usually accept credit cards, and a few of them even accept checks for payment. Unfortunately, the practice of accepting checks is becoming the exception to the rule, because so many people have tried to pass bad checks.

> ## Million $ Tip
>
> Search for "auction houses" in your state on the internet, because a lot of them have great auctions going on all the time. This includes doing storage unit auctions that they are hired to handle. The best tip I can give is to become friends with the managers of these auction houses, or get on their mailing list, so you can know when these auctions happen.

Many secondhand stores have limited budgets and closely monitor operating costs just to survive, so the practice of not accepting personal checks is becoming the norm. I suggest all my readers bring credit cards or cash. As far as credit cards go, bring your Visa or Mastercard, but not your American Express. You can leave that card at home. Why? As mentioned before, credit card companies charge the retailer transaction fees every time a credit card is used. It costs the retailer 2% to 4% of the purchase price on every sale, and American Express is the most expensive concerning fees.

When can you negotiate prices? If the secondhand store is a mom-and-pop type store, you can always try to negotiate the sales price. The worst thing the seller can say is no. Typically, the smaller the store, the more negotiating leeway. From my experience, large secondhand stores (for example, Goodwill or Salvation Army) rarely, if ever, negotiate. If you become friends with the manager and they see you all the time, then you might be able to negotiate.

Almost every major city has these types of secondhand stores— places packed with great items, valuable finds, and hidden treasures. They're yours for the taking! To locate the

Million $ Tip

Become friends with the managers of secondhand stores. They will give you great little tips, like when new shipments arrive and when the store will be restocked.

closest mom-and-pop secondhand stores, check listings on Nextdoor and Facebook, or try searching the internet. Always check the App Store for apps that can help in your treasure-hunting endeavors. To find some of the larger second-hand stores located near your community visit:

- **Goodwill Industry Stores**
  (www.goodwill.org/locator)
- **Salvation Army Thrift Stores**
  (www.salvationarmyusa.org)
- **AMVETS Thrift Stores**
  (www.amvetsnsf.org/stores.html)

Some of the main things you'll want to look for in secondhand stores are art, books, and china. For art items, check the walls, the back room, or anywhere else art could possibly be placed in the store. Small items, such as books and china, are usually scattered throughout the store. Many items considered valuable by the store owner are kept close to the front counter, in glass cases. But don't be fooled by their conspicuous placement; most of the items displayed in the cases have little value.

Many times, individuals will go into their parent's homes when they've recently passed away or moved into an assisted-living facility, taking anything and everything they can lay their hands on. Then it's off to the second- hand stores.

Although many of the items you find in second-hand stores carry no value whatsoever, there are some items of value to be found. I constantly hear stories of people finding items worth a great deal of money this way.

> ### Million $ Tip
>
> Don't just go to your local second-hand store. If you go to the stores in more expensive neighborhoods, there is a good chance you will find more valuable items.

Estate Auctions

Estate auctions might seem a bit intimidating to you since

you're bidding against other people, but this fear is totally unfounded. Not only are estate auctions a great deal of fun to attend, but you can also find some real treasures that can net you serious cash.

When a crowd of very excited individuals sets the price for all the items being auctioned in a room, you can bet your bottom dollar it's going to be an exciting day. Whether you're in a bidding war against a group of people or just with one other person, it's important to know why people bid an item up, so you can make sure you don't get caught up in the middle of an unnecessary bidding frenzy and wind up paying too much for an item.

> ### Million $ Tip
>
> Always be cautious about getting caught up in a bidding war. Most of the time, if you're not careful, you'll pay more than you want to, and you may actually pay more than the item is really worth.

Consider the following possibilities:

- These bidders know the real value of the item and they're willing to pay it.
- They have some sort of sentimental attachment to the item they're bidding on. Money is a secondary concern in these cases.
- They think there's a big value for the item for sale, but they have no clue whatsoever about its true worth.

Once you understand why people bid an item up, knowing as much as possible about the item is extremely important. If you truly do not understand what you're bidding on, you will get caught up in a bidding war and pay much more money than you should.

Knowing the way estate auctions work is also key. One of the best ways to understand how the process works is to attend as many estate actions as possible before you start actually bidding on anything. A major benefit of attending multiple estate auctions is that you'll learn how to pick out the professional bidders—the elite group that you'll soon become a part of, once you know how the system works.

> ### Million $Tip
>
> I always get helpful tips and tricks for auction hunting by watching *Antiques Roadshow* on PBS. The appraisers share tons of great information on what the experts are looking for in certain antiques.

These experienced bidders know exactly how to place the right bid at the right time and work the system so that the final auction price stays as low as possible. Also, by attending a lot of estate auctions, you can see what these pros are bidding on—so you can get an idea of what's valuable and what's not.

When you attend an auction, you'll need to be ready with the right method of payment. Know in advance what the preferred method of payment is at that particular auction. Cash is best for items up to a few thousand dollars. If you're going to be buying something in the ten-thousand-dollar range and up, it's probably best to make good use of your credit card for the payment. But by paying cash when you can for auction items,

> ### Million $Tip
>
> A secret for getting the best deal on items at an estate auction is to stay until it's over. People tend to leave auctions early, so some of the very best deals can be found closer to the end.

you'll save on credit card fees. (Some auction houses may charge you more if you use a credit card.) Auction houses usually do not take American Express, and many do not accept Discover Cards either. If you stick with Visa or Mastercard, you'll be just fine. As mentioned earlier, many auction houses do not accept personal checks due to the fraud issues associated with them. Again, it is imperative to call ahead to verify which payment options are accepted, because every auction house is different.

> ### Million $ Tip
>
> For a comprehensive, up-to-date, searchable database of estate sales in your area, visit www.estatesales.net.

Estate auctions can last just a couple of hours or be an all-day event. Set your schedule to afford yourself enough time in case the auction runs late. If the auction takes all day, make sure you bring extra food, snacks, and water. This may sound funny and may feel awkward at first, but many auctions don't have any type of concession stand available for their customers. If they do have one, prices are exorbitant, sometimes double what you might normally expect to pay. Also, check to see what the weather will be on the day of the auction. Some estate auctions are held outside or in warehouses that could be very hot or cold

> ### Million $ Tip
>
> If you are looking for estate sales/auctions look no further than AuctionNinja.com. It is a tech solution and online marketplace designed by estate sale pros for estate sale pros. This easy-to-use, affordable technology solution allows vendors to hold more sales than ever in a fraction of the time and with fewer resources.

depending on the time of year. Dress accordingly.

Storage Unit Auctions

When I talk about the most exciting treasure hunting out there, I'm talking about going to storage unit auctions. You may be asking, "Storage unit auctions? Are you serious? How can they be exciting? They're just storage units, right?" Well, they really are great fun, as I will explain. In every city, in every county, in every state in the country, millions upon millions of people use storage units to hold some, or most, of their belongings, due to a variety of circumstances. When people move, many times they need a place to store items. When they can't fit everything in their home or simply don't want to have their homes filled with clutter and unused items, they store their extra items at an external location.

> **Million $ Tip**
>
> Don't miss a chance to go to an auction if the weather is bad or if there's a big game on television. The fewer people who show up at an auction, the better chance for you to get the best deals!

Storage unit operators usually charge a monthly rental fee for the use of their space, and many times offer discounts if the customer signs up for the rental on an annual basis. If a customer fails to remain current on rental payments, lapses for 90 days, and doesn't respond to repeated calls or letters from the storage unit operators, by law, the contents of the unit can be auctioned off. Usually, the owner or manager of that specific location will put out auction advertisements, list the auction on their website, and continue their attempts to let the renter know that the contents of their unit are subject to a potential auction. Once a storage unit customer has reached the 90-day delinquent mark, an auction date is set, the auctioneer is called to the storage unit, and the bidding commences.

Million $ Tip

With the exposure from television shows about storage unit auctions, there's a good chance there will be a large crowd gathered at any auction. You should know that most of them are "looky-loos", so you needn't be intimidated by the size of the crowd. Usually, there's only a handful of actual bidders at every auction.

Once the bidding starts, it's up to you to look at the contents to see if you want to bid on the items contained in the storage unit. You will only have one to three minutes to take a look and, as I explain a little later, you will not be allowed to enter the unit. There could be only you and a few other people bidding on the contents, or there could be dozens of other individuals bidding. It's a crap shoot concerning what you may end up buying, and you need to be prepared for any situation.

Million $ Tip

Reality television shows like *Storage Wars* are not real: they are entertainment. Most units have very little value. Don't get me wrong— there are units out there that you can turn into a big pay day, but it is not the norm. With a storage unit auction, you have maybe a 1 in 25 chance of finding some good stuff.

Everyone at a storage unit auction is thinking the same

thing—they're going to find that big treasure and a huge payday. This is the point where the excitement begins. You really are going to have to put that excitement in check if you want to focus and score big at the auction.

Let's backtrack a bit to give you better insight into the storage unit auction process. As I mentioned before, you'll be given a short time to look at the contents. This is where the tools of the trade—those items I listed at the beginning of the chapter—come into play. The large, high-powered flashlight helps you get a good look at the contents tucked in the back of the unit.

Of course, there's a catch to viewing the contents: You can't break the door jamb. What does that mean? Your head cannot cross the threshold of the door to the storage unit. As I've already said, this process is a real crap shoot! If your head crosses this line, the auctioneer will shout at you. Truth be told, I've gotten yelled at on more than one occasion!

This is where the selfie stick enters the fray. I like to use a selfie stick with my phone attached and on video mode, so I can get a good look at what is wedged way in the back of the storage unit. Practice with it so you can quickly get a look.

Million $Tip

When bidding at a storage unit auction, stay calm and avoid getting swept up in the excitement. Since you can't enter the unit or see everything inside, focus on observing what's visible and estimating its value. Use this information to make an educated guess about the worth of the unseen items.

When it comes to bidding on the contents, only about10% of the crowd bidders will drop out. When it comes to the end of the bidding, usually it will be you and one other person. This is really when you must put your emotions in check. If you don't you could wind up paying much more than the contents are actually worth.

Additionally, you will need to calculate the time it will take to clear out the unit if you are the person with the winning bid. You need to consider not only the money you spend to win the auction but also the total amount of time you'll need to spend throughout the entire process. It's beneficial, and a huge time saver, if you can find someone to help you empty the unit. Family members or good friends are the best helpers. Plus, they usually work cheaply! For the price of a trip to Starbucks or McDonalds, you'll usually get all the help you need. Along with your helpers, you need to have a trailer or large vehicle available, so you can get all the goods you've purchased removed quickly within the allotted time.

Million $Tip

You must consider your ability to sell what's in the unit. When people see antiques, they're going to start bidding the price up immediately. Unfortunately, antiques are no longer the huge money-makers they once were! While some antiques are very valuable, the market is oversaturated. Ultimately, you must place a limit on what you're willing to spend on the unit.

If everything goes well and you've won the bid, now what? Usually, you'll have 24 to 48 hours to remove everything in the unit and leave it completely empty. If you feel you're unable to clean out the unit within this time limit, then you'll need to rent the space for a month.

I strongly recommend this course of action. There's nothing worse than knowing you are under the gun and cannot get the storage unit cleaned out in time. By renting the space for just a month, you will save on having to pay the deposit money, which is usually between $50 and $75, and you'll have more time to find a place to store all the treasures you've just acquired.

Million $ Tip

If you don't have enough cash to pay for your storage unit auction winnings approximately thirty minutes after the auction closes, the storage unit operator will re-auction the unit, and you will lose your claim on all items in the unit.

Don't buy the contents of the storage unit and then go home and think about it. You'll want to clean out the contents of the storage unit immediately. Get it done ASAP, as time could be of the essence if there are treasures that need to be resold promptly. You certainly don't want to miss your window of opportunity if a potential buyer for your new acquisitions goes elsewhere because you procrastinated.

Large plastic bags for trash are handy, as well as a wheelbarrow, dolly, cart— anything you can load items on and move them to your vehicle. Most times, you won't be able to back up to a storage unit. Many franchise storage facilities are located indoors. Obstacles may include elevators or stairs used to get to and from the unit. The easier you make it for yourself, the faster you can remove your new-found cache from the unit.

In my many years of buying and selling items recovered from storage units, I've seen everything, ranging from furniture and kitchenware to personal items, like clothing and important documents—even food. You name it, I've seen it!

Many storage unit operators recommend that, if you find something of a very personal nature, such as a birth certificate, you attempt to return it to the unit operator and ask that they get it to the rightful owner. I think this is a great idea; some of the personal items discovered in these units are of no value to you but are irreplaceable to the person who lost them.

Also, be prepared to find metal objects in a storage unit. There may be items you can sell for the metal weight, such as copper, silver, or even gold. You'll find many tools as well. Tools have a huge amount of resale value, and many people will bid on the unit if they see tools as part of the contents. Additional items to seek out in a storage unit are televisions and computers. There's a catch here though. Many of these items could be obsolete and have little to no resale value. You should never place much value on older computers and televisions. These items may not work, or newer versions have been produced at much cheaper prices. Don't let obsolete electronics distract you when you're looking through a unit.

You will likely find a lot of trash, so always be prepared for that. You'll find many items in a storage unit that have no real market value and can be easily donated to Goodwill or the Salvation Army. If you don't need an item, donate it. You'll be helping families in need, and you might be able to use your donations as a tax write-off.

Million $ Tip

If you discover anything you believe is illegal, call the police right away. You do not want to be a part of any crime! Simply call the police and advise them you just brought the contents of the unit. They will completely understand and you will not be charged with anything criminal.

Storage unit auctions move very quickly. Units can sell in just a few minutes. Storage unit operators want to move quickly to get the unit's contents sold so they can make money from the next renter of the space. Auctions can include a single unit up to fifteen units being auctioned off all at once. You'll want to make sure you have the money to bid on all of them; you never know what's in the next unit since only one is shown and auctioned off at a time. You'll never get to look through all of them first before deciding which unit or units you want to bid on.

As mentioned earlier, make sure to bring cash. Credit cards and personal checks are rarely accepted. What happens when you run out of cash and don't have the money to cover your purchase? Hopefully, you can leave for a few moments and run to an ATM, your bank, or call a friend or relative to bring you more cash.

To find out where the auctions are in your area, search the internet for storage unit auctions in your city. When you locate the storage unit operators you want to do business with, get on their email list so they can send you alerts when auctions will take place. This is the easiest way to get advance notice of auction dates and times, as well as locations, and the number of units to be auctioned. In case you don't receive the emails, always double-check the company's website; many storage unit operators post their auctions online.

Garage Sales

Attending garage and yard sales as a buyer and running them as a seller are how I got started in the collecting business a long time ago. With garage sales and yard sales being similar in nature, I will just refer to them from this point forward as garage sales.

Way back when I was putting on garage sales with my mother and learning the value of the goodies we were putting out to sell, frequent garage sale goers would tell us we should raise our prices on this or lower our prices on that. I am grateful to have received their knowledge and experience. Imagine the countless other garage sales where people not only have no clue what their stuff is worth, but they may not even know what they are selling! It happens all the time.

Million $Tip

If there's a garage sale you think is going to be a blockbuster, go to the house the night before and offer them $20 to get a look at what they'll be selling. This will save you time and effort for the next day. If you see something good, you might want to try negotiating right then and there.

The main component of any garage sale, besides the buying and selling of items, is negotiating every sale. As a buyer, you never want to pay the asking price. If you are not negotiating every sale, you are wasting your money.

I've run garage sales in the past where I put the sale sign up and someone was at my front door waiting for me before I even got back from putting up the sign. People absolutely *love* searching through garage sales for things they may need or want to own. As a Garage Sale Millionaire, you're going hunting with the express intent of finding items you believe to have a high resale value—items that will make you lots of money!

If the garage sale begins at 9:00 AM, you want to be there and ready to go at 8:30 AM. Don't be at all surprised if other people, wanting to get a jump on the crowd, arrive at the sale before it's scheduled to begin.

There is a great deal of time and stress expended in the preparation of hosting a garage sale. You must make certain everything is laid out and displayed the way you like. Items need to be labeled, and prices need to be set correctly to guarantee you're getting the maximum sale value possible.

> **Million $ Tip**
>
> To get the best deals at garage sales, go early and go often. Hit garage sales when they start and go to as many sales as possible. Also try to visit close to closing time. Great deals will be even better!

People often forget they have items they want to sell and forget to put them out. One of the keys to a successful garage sale is to take your time in the days before your sale and make sure everything is accounted for regarding what you want to sell. The adage "the early bird gets the worm" applies perfectly to garage sales. By arriving early for a garage sale, the savvy garage sale buyer gets the jump on the competition by being able to see everything laid out, ready to purchase, before others arrive. The only reason you would show up at the end of a garage sale is if the seller had something good at the onset, but the item was priced way too high.

If you show up during the last moments of any sale and make a low-ball offer on the items you're looking for, the seller may take your offer knowing he or she won't be getting any others. If you don't want to drive back to the garage sale as it nears completion, you could try and get the name and telephone number of the seller before you take off, then call back at the end of the sale to see if they still have the item in which you were interested. Most sellers will gladly give out their name and telephone number.

Million $ Tip

When you are at a garage sale, just because an item is not out does not mean it is not for sale. You need to ask the seller about items you are specifically looking for— antique chairs, old photographs, old baseball cards, pretty much anything in which you are interested. Ask them very politely and you never know what you may be able to get!

A great way to view garage sales around your area is to use the internet. By using specific search terms, there's a great chance a website will pop up with sales listed in your area. Community-oriented apps like Facebook Marketplace, NextDoor, and Craigslist are great places to check for upcoming sales. It's truly amazing how popular garage sales really are!

Another way of locating garage sales is to drive

around to as many neighborhoods as you can on Friday night or Saturday morning. People will begin putting out signs for their sales during this time.

Whenever you attend a garage sale, be prepared so that you don't pay more for an item than you should. If you have a smartphone, you can search the internet and track down the value of an item. As I will discuss in detail later in the book, a good place for determining value is eBay.

When you're trying to research items very quickly, be certain to take the extra few moments needed to match apples to apples. For example, if you just found an original Star Wars Kenner Darth Vader action figure in near-mint condition from the 1970s at a neighborhood garage sale, and it is being sold on eBay for $2,495, make sure the action figure at the garage sale matches the eBay listing exactly. You would hate to find out, when you got home, that the $375 cash you just spent on an item you thought was valued at $2,500 ended up being a "Star Wars ROTJ Darth Vader figure MOC KENNER" action figure from 1993, valued on eBay at only $55.

Million $ Tip

To assist in the pricing of used books, try one of the many "live scanning" apps for iPhone or Android. With these, you can use your device's camera to scan a barcode. The apps utilize your mobile data to retrieve pricing information from Amazon, or other online sources.
Most of these apps are free (**Amazon Seller App, Scoutify, and eBay**), and the highest rated, **Profit Bandit**.

When buying at a garage sale, it's definitely caveat emptor: buyer beware. You need to make sure you're happy with whatever item you buy. Try to do your due diligence and research on the spot. If you're not happy with the item for any reason, don't buy it. There is a no return, no refund policy at almost every garage sale. This is true even if you walk to your car, turn right back around, and try to return your purchase immediately. You'll be stuck because all sales are final. That's one of the main reasons why garage sales are operated on a cash-only basis.

The Salvation Army Thrift Stores, Goodwill Industry stores, and other secondhand stores will not refund the selling price either, but they may give you store credit. Store policies may differ from location to location, so be sure to check these policies before making your purchase. You must always buy things with the understanding that you are not going to be able to get your money back, even if you decide to return an item.

There is no harm in bringing collectible resource books along to help you make your final choices at a garage sale. No one will say anything negative if you have a coin book in one hand and an antique book in the other. This is just what a smart and savvy Garage Sale Millionaire does: they arrive prepared!

Million $ Tip

Set maximums to avoid overpaying and focus on profitable items. Use your target profit, like $25 per sale or a 10% margin, as a guide. However, stay flexible and seize opportunities that guarantee significant returns, even if they exceed your limits. For example, buying for $5,000 and selling for $6,000 ensures a strong profit. Stay alert during auctions, as unexpected treasures can lead to great paydays. Ultimately, this approach will maximize your profits.

Auctions

Auctions occur all the time, with frequency depending on the size of the auction house. Auction houses now hold multiple auctions every week. They are easily found by looking online. There are several sites you can check, such as **Christie's, Sotheby's, Phillips, Bonhams,** and **Heritage Auctions.** By taking advantage of various online auction websites, you can sign up to be continuously notified about happenings in your area. Search online for local auction listings, then subscribe to as many email lists as you can find. Another fantastic place to find auctions is on **AuctionZip** (www.auctionzip.com) and **Bidsquare** (www.bidsquare.com), both of which have apps.

Don't confuse regular auctions with estate auctions—they are completely different. An auction is a public sale of property that is sold to the highest bidder. With an estate auction, all merchandise is valued by an appraiser, priced accordingly, and sold on a first-come, first-serve basis. At auctions or estate auctions, anything and everything could be auctioned off to a lucky high bidder.

Items at a regular auction may include entire inventories from an auto parts store, valuable (and not-so-valuable) coins, used cooking equipment from a restaurant, television or movie memorabilia, old tractors, antiques, guns, or home theater equipment. You need to personally determine what auction is interesting to you, and potentially profitable.

Besides the crowd that sets the auction prices, the most interesting facet of the auction process to me is that an auction can be held anywhere. They can be held in the capital of your state or the smallest rural towns. The auctions held in small remote areas are the ones you definitely want to go to frequently. If it's difficult for you to get there, it's equally difficult for everyone else. The fewer people attend an auction, the better chance there is for you to get a fantastic deal.

For every auction, there will usually be an online listing describing what will be auctioned off. Some auctions also hold preview days, where you can show up at the auction location to look at everything that will be going up for sale.

Preview days usually take place 48 to 72 hours before the start of the auction. Taking advantage of preview days and asking questions about the items on the auction block are very important aspects of the auction process. Why? Because you can get an in-depth idea and understanding of what is up for sale, make detailed notes about what's going to be auctioned off, and do valuable research on the actual value of the items being offered before the auction begins. By taking advantage of the preview days, you can also view any item, make sure it hasn't been damaged or poorly restored, and ensure it has all the necessary parts and packaging— whatever it takes to make the item worth the highest amount of money possible.

If you can't attend the auction preview days in person, give the company holding the auction (usually an auction house) a call if you have any questions. If you're interested in a big-ticket item, you need to examine it personally. The person helping you on the phone is not an expert, and they have no skin in the game if they make a mistake.

You will also need to set your top end price on items before the auction. If you do not complete your due diligence and research on the items you're interested in owning, you can easily overpay for them. I've seen so many people overpay for auction items over the years that I lost count decades ago. It doesn't happen once or twice; it happens at every single auction. I've seen people pay many times over the retail price for items being auctioned. However, the key to becoming a Garage Sale Millionaire is being able to find those hidden treasures and pay less than their value so you can turn a profit when you resell them.

If you are bidding against someone or a group of bidders, you should know there are usually three reasons why people bid on an item:

1. **People think the item is more valuable than the current bid.** At some point during every auction, people will believe they are way ahead of the curve and that the current auction bid on an item, or set of items, is undervalued. This usually occurs when due diligence is not done before the beginning of an auction. You would be surprised at how many people believe they know what an item is really worth when, in reality, they have no clue. This happens all the time. These are the moments when you can really clean up as a Garage Sale Millionaire. If the bidding doesn't reach the actual value of an item, you can win the bid and make a fantastic profit upon resale. If the bidding goes way above the actual value of an item, and you have done the proper research on the item, you won't overpay for something.

2. **The item has some kind of personal meaning to the bidder.** When you're bidding against someone who has an emotional attachment to an item, it's definitely not about money. These bidders want to

have the item at any cost. They usually have the means and bankroll to buy any item they desire. You need to watch out for this kind of bidder because it will cost you big if you're not ready. You're thinking they know something about the item when, in reality, they know nothing about the item, and just want it because it has some degree of personal meaning or importance to them. When you get caught up in a bidding war against this type of bidder, you can go way upside down on an item and pay too much. How can you spot this type of person? Before an auction begins, people linger around the items they are interested in and are very chatty about what's going to be up for auction. Listen closely to what seems to be innocuous and innocent banter, as it could give you great insight and save you money when the bidding begins! During the bidding, also pay careful attention to how people are bidding, and how emotionally attached they seem to be to certain items. Are they excited? Are their eyes wider than normal? Are they unusually attentive? Does their posture—the way they carry themselves—appear as though they're excited about something that's happening? All these signs suggest they may have more than a passing interest in what is up for sale at the auction.

3. **They think there's big value in the item for sale but have no clue whatsoever about the item's true value.** These are spur-of-the- moment buyers who saw the item on eBay or in another auction and feel that they're experienced enough to bid on it. These bidders can be dangerous at an auction because they start quickly bidding up items

without the knowledge to back up their numbers. This is why you must have a ceiling when bidding: spur-of-the-moment bidders could run the cost of an item up to two or three times more than its actual value and they won't realize their mistake until they get home and do their research. If you do your research before the auction and place a mental ceiling on what you are willing to pay, you will always be protected.

I was at an auction a few years ago and wanted to win a particular item very badly. It was an old vase I saw that had very interesting markings. I found out about the auction at the last minute so, unfortunately, I did not have time to research the item. However, I did place a ceiling on what I was willing to pay.

A woman began bidding against me, and the bidding quickly escalated. Everyone except the two of us dropped out of the bidding for the vase. I made an exception to my own rule as I kept making bids above my ceiling. As I said, I really wanted this item! As a result, I got unnecessarily caught up in the heightened level of excitement. Unfortunately for me, she kept on making higher and higher bids. By this time, I was way above my ceiling and had to end my bidding and bow out. To my chagrin, she eventually ended up buying the item.

After the auction, I approached her and asked her what she thought was so important about this vase. She told me she knew nothing about the vase, but she had described it to her mother over the telephone and her mother was extremely interested in acquiring this piece. I further inquired as to why her mother was so interested in this particular item. It was because her mom had a similar vase at home that was irreparably damaged. Her mother simply thought this vase could easily replace the broken one. She had no idea what the vase was worth, and she didn't care. She just had to have the vase.

I guarantee you that, once you begin attending auctions, you'll start seeing the same faces at almost every auction. Many people do this for a living and attend auctions weekly, like clockwork. These are the people who will also drop out of the bidding quickly when the bidding goes too high. If you want an item more than they do, they will see this, and stop bidding when the price rises above their ceiling.

When I talk to my customers, I find out all the time that people are intimidated and afraid of the magical, mystical bidding process at an auction. Some people think, like they see in the shows and movies, that they have to do something very elaborate, like tweak their nose or pull their ear, to even take part in an auction. This couldn't be further from the truth. All you have to do is take your bid number, which is provided to you at the start of the auction, and raise it in the air. This is always the accepted sign that you are bidding on an item. It's that simple.

Correctly bidding on and buying an item at an auction separates the successful Garage Sale Millionaire from the wannabes and the money-earners from the money-losers.

Along with completing your due diligence and research, and determining what items to bid on based on the profit you want to make, you also need to consider your costs. Costs throughout this process include three factors:

> **Time**—Time is money. The time it takes you to research an item, determine how much to charge for an item, sell the item, and collect payment all

factor into the time equation. The more time you spend on something, the more your actual profit diminishes. If you sell something for $4,500 that cost you $4,000, and it took you nearly 40 hours to sell it, that does not sound like it was a win-win. To me, it sounds more like a lose-lose situation. You need to figure time into your bottom line because it directly affects profit.

Auction House Premiums—Whenever you win something at an auction, you're going to be charged a buyer's premium by the auction house. A buyer's premium is a fee, charged by the auction house in addition to your winning bid amount. In higher-end auction houses, such as Sotheby's and Christie's, there's a very good chance you will be charged a fee ranging anywhere between 12% and 24%. In smaller auction houses, the premiums are a little less. Unfortunately for the buyer, all auction houses have a buyer's premium, as this is how they make their money and stay in business. Sellers also pay the same type of premium less. Unfortunately for the buyer, all auction houses have a buyer's premium, as this is how they make their money and stay in business. Sellers also pay the same type of premium or fee, called a seller's premium. These premiums are also steep and can range from 10% to 25%. If you ever wondered how auction houses stay profitable, now you know.

Sales Tax License—Earlier in the chapter, I discussed the benefits of having a sales tax license. Sales tax licenses are easily obtained and can potentially save you money. Again, the cost of acquiring a sales tax license is approximately $10 to $100.

Every auction house has slightly different rules regarding payment. As mentioned earlier, credit cards and cash are usually universally accepted forms of payment, whereas the practice of accepting personal checks is becoming rarer over time. Some

> **Million $ Tip**
>
> www.maxsold.com has great deals. It is also great for quick liquidation.

auction houses take checks, but many do not. I recommend calling ahead and inquiring about the acceptable payment options.

Almost every auction house takes credit cards as a form of payment. By using a credit card to pay for your auction wins, you can keep track of your financial activity in much greater detail than by solely using cash to make your purchases. Credit cards also have some level of theft protection, so if your card gets stolen you will usually be protected. Please check with your credit card issuer to determine, and verify, what level of protection you have, as every card is different.

Many credit cards have some type of mileage rewards program, so after a long week of buying at auctions, you will receive rewards points as well. Visa and Mastercard are usually accepted. Remember, American Express is typically not; sometimes Discover Card is not accepted either. So, it pays to check out what is accepted in advance.

Carrying a lot of cash around presents problems. I'm not talking about $50 or $60 in your wallet, but many hundreds, or thousands, of dollars in cash. Cash can be lost or stolen, and once it's gone, it's gone. If you don't have to carry cash, don't. Use your credit card.

For an exhaustive list of auctions, by category, visit **The National Auction List** (www.dealbid.com). Please keep in mind that many times auction houses hold auctions covering many categories. For example, **Heritage Auction Galleries** (www.ha.com) holds multiple auctions in the areas of art, comics, currency, entertainment memorabilia, historical items, movie posters, natural history items, rare books, and sports collectibles. Some of the major companies in the auction business are:

Art	Art Brokerage Christie's Sotheby's	www.artbrokerage.com www.christies.com www.sothebys.com/en
Automotive	Gooding & Company Barrett-Jackson Mecum Auto Auctions RM	www.goodingco.com/ www.barrett-jackson.com www.mecum.com www.rmsothebys.com
Baseball/Trading Cards	Baseball-Cards.com Memory Lane Inc.	www.baseball-cards.com www.memorylaneinc.com
Books	Rare Book Hub PBA Galleries Quinn's Auction Galleries	www.rarebookhub.com www.pbagalleries.com www.quinnsauction.com
Coins	Stack's Bowers Spink	www.stacksbowers.com www.spink.com
Comics	Comic Book Auction Ltd. Mile High Comics	www.compalcomics.com www.milehighcomics.com
Consumer Electronics	AudiogoN Heritage Auction Galleries	www.audiogon.com www.ha.com
Entertainment Memorabilia	Premiere Props Heritage Auctions	www.premiereprops.com www.ha.com

Firearms	Gun Broker	www.gunbroker.com
	Bonham's	www.bonhams.com/us
	Christie's	www.christies.com
	Freeman's Auction	www.freemansauction.com
	Heritage Auctions	www.ha.com
	Neal Auctions	www.nealauction.com
	Sotheby's	www.sothebys.com
Online	eBay	www.ebay.com
Sports Memorabilia	Leland's	www.lelands.com
	Robert Edward Auctions	www.robertedwardauctions.com
	SCP Auctions	www.scpauctions.com
Toys	Smith House Toys	www.smithhousetoys.com
	Theriaults	www.theriaults.com
	Toyzine	www.toyzine.com
Wine & Cigars	Acker Wines	www.ackerwines.com
	The Chicago Wine Co.	www.tcwc.com
	Cigar Auctioneer	www.cigarauctioneer.com
	HDH Wine	www.hdhwine.com
	Wine Bid	www.winebid.com
	Zachy's Auctions	auction.zachys.com/

Antique Stores

Antique stores are fascinating to visit. There are thousands of these shops across the country and, in some locations, there are also huge conglomerates housing multiple antique stores and booths in the same location. Each booth or store is usually owned or rented by a different individual or company. I like to go to antique stores in small towns as well as big cities because there are wonderful treasures to be found in both. Even where you there aren't many antique stores, like in the tourist cities of Santa Barbara, California, or Gettysburg, Pennsylvania, there are actually many of these shops to browse and shop to your heart's content.

When visiting an antique store, don't think that, just

because there are seemingly knowledgeable people behind the front desk, proper research has been done on every item on the floor. People make mistakes all the time. Sometimes big mistakes can work in your favor. It's up to you to search out which items are priced incorrectly. When you find those mistakes—and hopefully it will be a big mistake in your favor—make an immediate offer on the item. You might go home with a gem of a find that will net big money upon resale.

Million $ Tip

Some antique furniture has been unscrupulously replicated and, as a result, people are paying more for things they believe are correctly labeled as authentic antiques, when they are not. Unfortunately, I see newly manufactured furniture being disguised as old and labeled antique much more often at conglomerate warehouse antique stores. Overall, most vendors are honest and place a sign on the item advising that it is, indeed, a replica. Of course, there are always some vendors who are not so honest. Always be on the alert when you go to antique stores. It is extremely easy to make something look old and worth much more money than it truly is.

I've gone to some wonderful antique stores in my time, and have seen some really tantalizing items being sold. Some of the antiques are fairly accurately priced, others not so much. If I befriend the manager or store owner while I'm in their store, I'll usually learn more from them (not to mention there's a better chance I can make a deal on any item I find). It doesn't hurt to ask questions. I highly recommend it.

Always make an offer on anything you're interested in buying. In these tough economic times, I've not seen a reasonable offer rejected at an antique store. Sellers need to make quick sales so their business will survive. When you go into an antique store, look around and take your time. If you find an item you like, negotiate. Quite a few antique stores will take credit cards but, if you pay in cash, you might be able to get a better deal. Just like second-hand stores, antique stores prefer taking cash for a sale; they save money by not having to pay credit card transaction fees.

The Online Marketplace

There are many places online where you can find new or used items. The internet is full of websites where people can buy and resell personal items for a profit. Since attending garage sales continues to be an increasingly popular activity, it's only natural that this garage sale-type activity has evolved onto the internet.

With so many places to buy and sell goods online, it's an essential business strategy to choose the most successful from among all of the websites listed in this chapter. When you do business online, you have the best chance of success if you can make the most money possible as a seller, and save as much money as possible as a buyer.

There are a couple of websites that have not only stood the test of time but are still thriving in an extremely challenging economy. These three websites are considered the heavy hitters of the online marketplace: Craigslist, eBay, and Facebook Marketplace.

Craigslist

One of the websites that first comes to mind when discussing superior online marketplaces is **Craigslist** (www.craigslist.org). Craigslist is the most amazing online shopping experience I could ever imagine. It began operations in 1995 and originated as a bulletin board type message service to help people around San Francisco, California find things to do. Today, the company has grown into a global marketplace reaching all 50 United States (including Washington, DC), with a presence in 70 countries. Craigslist also has great companion apps available for download.

The items offered on Craigslist change every minute of every day. The most recent listing is on the top of the webpage. In as short a time as 30 seconds, listings will dramatically change, and brand-new listings will be posted. If you want to find some great items that will make you money, it's very important to check the website often throughout the day. If you see something you want to purchase, email the seller immediately.

Business transactions on Craigslist happen extremely quickly. If you don't act in a timely matter, which could be measured from minutes to hours, there's a strong possibility you'll lose an item to other individuals out there—just like you—who are trying to make money on this website. As with all online activities, don't let your guard down when it comes to conducting business. Always be on guard when you're thinking of parting with your money by making a purchase, or when you're ready to accept payment for an item you're going to sell. As a buyer, there are several ways to protect yourself when doing business on Craigslist. If you're conducting business with someone locally, don't send any money to the seller until you see the item of interest. Arrange to meet the seller in a public place to look at the item whenever possible. In my experience, a local coffee shop seems to be the best place to meet the seller.

Million $ Tip

Many local police departments now participate in **SafeTrade**, a program that provides safe, neutral spaces for buyers and sellers to meet. Some stations reserve parking spaces in their lot, monitored by cameras, while others invite the community to conduct business in their lobbies. For helpful tips on where, when, and how to safely carry out transactions, as well as a list of participating police stations in your area, visit www.safetradestations.com.

If you do business with someone from another state, try to get as much background information as possible (i.e. a detailed description of the item, multiple pictures of the item, and any history that comes along with the item). It is not that buying on Craigslist from a different part of the United States is a bad thing. Deals can be made. It's just a bit trickier. If you are the seller of an item, the ways to protect yourself when doing business on Craigslist are pretty much the same as they are for a buyer. This means, when conducting business locally, always verify the item in question, and personally meet the buyer in a (preferably) public place to get payment on the item.

The best payment option when conducting business on Craigslist is cash. Almost every time I've sold items on the website, the buyer pays in cash. Because people usually sell their items locally, people expect to pay cash for whatever they buy. Be wary of accepting cashier's checks or certified checks. They can easily be counterfeited. It's better to meet the person face to face and ask for cash for your item. If you sell to someone outside of your area, such as another state or country, make sure the payment you receive clears the bank and funds are verified before sending the merchandise. If you can't meet someone in person to exchange funds, use **PayPal** (www.paypal.com) Goods & Services.

Million $ Tip

If a buyer wants to send you a money order for more than your asking price and asks you to give the difference to the person who picks up the item... this is a scam! You will lose your item and "the difference," and be left with nothing but a worthless, fraudulent money order for your trouble.

Remember, when looking for items on Craigslist, listings change very rapidly, and there is always something of interest to buy. Also, do not limit your search to the state in which you live. As previously mentioned, there are Craigslist's for cities all over the world. If you live in California, take a look at what's being sold in New York. Searching these lists can consume hours each day but, when you find that rare hidden treasure, all your efforts will be worth it.

Many of my friends who buy items at secondhand stores, thrift stores, storage unit sales, estate auctions, and garage sales will put those items on Craigslist to move them quickly, so they can get their cash back along with a profit as soon as possible. My friends also note that they'll list items for less on Craigslist than they would elsewhere because they want to move them quickly. Don't ever be afraid to make a counteroffer on items you're interested in buying on the website. Talk to the seller, make the counteroffer, and you never know what you might get for less money than you ever expected to spend!

eBay

Everyone who has a computer—and even those who don't—knows about eBay. Over the years, eBay has managed to make its way into the popular vernacular as the default term for buying and selling anything on the internet. eBay is where more items are bought and sold than any other single location in the world, with a reach spanning over 30 countries. I've dedicated Chapter 6 entirely to eBay to explore this website in greater detail.

I sell a lot of items on eBay each month. As a business person, eBay has opened up avenues I could never have imagined for my art and collectibles gallery. The same opportunities I have as a former gallery owner and private collector to sell my treasure globally are also easily afforded to you. With a straightforward user interface, tens of millions of users with hundreds of millions of items listed for sale, and a support community that helps buyers and sellers alike, eBay is the best place to get your items noticed and to make a handsome profit.

Facebook Marketplace

The only website here that could possibly dwarf eBay by comparison would, of course, be the origin of social media itself: **Facebook** (www.facebook.com). With the rapid development of Facebook in the last 10 years or so, there's been a flood of new features on the platform, including social media gaming and a sophisticated tagging system for locations, people, and events. We can even show people what we are watching on TV. Now there is **Facebook** **Marketplace** (www.facebook.com/marketplace/), a platform for you to sell your goods to your friends, and their friends, across social media.

Facebook Marketplace works a lot like old-school free classified ads; you can post your unwanted goods with the hope a buyer will come by with cash in hand. Facebook utilizes the "social" aspect of social media to reach an audience near you, which is based on rough location confirmations when you post your items for sale. Many sellers have reported selling things almost instantly on Facebook Marketplace to local groups, while the same items would sit unsold on eBay.

Selling items on Facebook Marketplace has some great benefits. First, it's free to use—while eBay can take away up to 10% of your sale in fees—Facebook Marketplace is a little to no-risk endeavor for any seller. The Marketplace is also very easy to use, as most people use Facebook, and the operations of the Marketplace are just as user-friendly and thoughtfully explained. There's also the ability to post items in a quick fashion, which saves you time (and money) in your Garage Sale Millionaire efforts!

The drawbacks of using the Marketplace are minimal, but knowing about them in advance will make any trek through the Facebook Marketplace a lot simpler. The group pages within the Marketplace are often run by volunteer administrators, not professional dealers or paid staff, and Facebook as a company will NOT get involved with transactions between buyers and sellers—this means you're on your own if there's a problem or dispute over a sale. Also, if you live in a rural area, you won't reach as many people as you could in a more urban area, as Facebook Marketplaces operates off proximity to your location. Keep those points in mind before posting sales to the Marketplace!

Million $Tip

Another great tool for researching collectibles online is **Google's Reverse Image Search** (www.images.google.com). Open a new image search on your browser, then click the camera icon in the search bar. You can either upload a file, drag-and-drop it, or paste a link to a photo online, then search. Google will pull millions of its "best guesses" for related images, allowing you to conduct a visual search for similar items, complete with convenient links to other useful sites and selling platforms. You can use this tool effectively with most web browsers, but there are a few perks to accessing it within Google Chrome, Google's web browser. For example, if you have an image open in Chrome and want to research similar items, or follow the image back to its source, you can simply right click on the picture and select "Search Google for the image." You can also do this on the **eBay** app to search their inventory for similar items to the one you have.

When you get started with posting sales on Facebook Marketplace, you'll need these tips and tricks to get the most out of your time and effort. Be sure you join groups early on! Just search your area or post code in the main search box, alongside words such as "selling," "sale," or "buy". Join as many as you can even in areas bordering you, to increase your sales radius—and don't limit yourself to just sales groups. Be sure to browse through special interest groups for specific hobbies or activities; just be sure that the rules of the group allow you to post items for sale before doing so.

Remember that posts you make on Facebook Marketplace, no matter where they are, are public. Whenever you're posting items for sale, whether it be your own page or a group page, be sure you are keeping your listing to a general location versus an exact address. Safety first when you're on the internet! When you're posting your item descriptions, be sure to follow the rules of any page you are posting on and include detailed photos you've taken of the items.

When negotiating sales through Facebook Marketplace, remember that most of the negotiating should take place within a private message, either on the Facebook Messenger app or through the Messenger window within Facebook's online portal. This will keep any private information secure from the public. Keep your sales limited to cash/Venmo/PayPal/etc., as a check can so easily be a scam. Facebook Marketplace isn't the place to post incredibly expensive items, like rare artwork or historical artifacts, so cash should be alright for smaller items that are easily valued. Maintain a strict 24-hour time limit on holding items for sale in the event a selected buyer is unresponsive or needs time to come up with the payment you both agreed on. Make sure you communicate this, both in the advertising posts you've created and in any personal messages with the potential buyer.

If you are going to advertise and do well on Facebook Marketplace, you must take great photos of the item you are posting. Making sure exact measurements are included is vital. It is also important to list if the packaging is included and take pictures of it. If it comes with any warranty or brochures then list that too. Include how much use the item has gotten or if it is new. Make sure you try to price the item using the completed auction section on eBay to get a rough idea of what the item sold for last. You will want to price your item 20-50% less than that sold price. The reason for this is, that items on Facebook Marketplace go for a lot cheaper than on eBay. Facebook Marketplace is a great place to sell furniture, clothing, decor, and lower-end items under $1000 that are too difficult to ship. eBay is your best bet if it's easy to ship to a national or international audience, like coins, jewelry, and collectibles.

The biggest downside to Facebook Marketplace is the number of scams. To work around these, you need to be extra vigilant. Here are the biggest things to look for:

- *When someone asks a question about your item, make sure you look at their profile.* Make sure that they have one and that it's been up for a while. Also, check that they have a reasonable number of friends.

- *If they ask for your phone number, they are going to try to clone or copy your profile.* Believe it or not, they can do a lot of damage with just your phone number alone. Scammers will also try to have a code sent to your phone to "verify" your identity before you buy/sell an item. If you share the code with them, they will use it to access one of your accounts or create a fake account in your name. If someone sends you a verification code when you are trying to buy or sell an item, delete it, report it, and block them.

- NEVER ACCEPT CHECKS OR OVERPAY FOR AN ITEM. There is a scam where they ask to write you a check or ask you to send money to a Venmo/ CashApp account for more than the item is worth, and a delivery driver will come get the item and you give the driver the difference to pay for the delivery. In most cases, they will also give you more than you are asking for the item and call it an inconvenience fee. When it comes to Facebook Marketplace, PayPal Goods & Services is going to be the best way to go.

Another scam is that you will see a friend of yours trying to sell an item directly on their page, not through the marketplace. When you contact them and tell them you want what they have to offer, they will try to talk to you very quickly. The items will be well-priced and they will haggle a little bit to make everything look legit. However, when you agree to a price, they will tell you that you need to PayPal a friend or a relative of theirs. The PayPal account will most likely look suspicious. In this case, someone has cloned the whole Facebook account and you are talking to a scammer and not your friend.

If you use PayPal, always use their Goods & Services feature instead of paying through Friends & Family. To do this, select the "Paying for an item or service" option when you send a payment. There is a fee associated with this, but this option protects buyers from scams, so in my professional opinion, the fee is worth it. If an eligible item that you've bought online doesn't arrive or doesn't match the seller's description, then PayPal will reimburse you for the full purchase amount of the item plus postage. This can be a great tell whether or not someone is scamming you because if they are not willing to use the Goods & Services feature, they are most likely not legit.

A common scam that is run is a scammer pretending to be an employee of a payment provider in an attempt to gain your personal details. This can be an employee of Venmo, CashApp, Zelle, or any other payment provider.

Avoid giving out any personal details unless you are absolutely sure you are talking to a legitimate employee. But most often, employees of these providers will not reach out to you through anything but email. If you do receive an email from something that looks legit, always verify the email address it came from. If you ever have any doubt, the best thing to do is call the payment provider and ask them if they actually need any personal

In summary, the best ways to avoid scams on Facebook Marketplace is to only communicate using Facebook, avoid anything that seems too good to be true, use trusted payment providers, and don't deal with high-pressure buyers/sellers.

With these tips, you'll be selling more things than you ever thought possible, all through the power of social media!

Amazon

Amazon (www.amazon.com) is one of the most trusted brands in the U.S. It is not widely realized, but independent sellers actually make up more than 60% of sales in the Amazon store. Amazon is the best place, in my opinion, to sell things in bulk. If you buy a storage unit in an auction for example, and you find a box filled with 1000 brand-new keychains in it, this would be a perfect item to sell on Amazon.

In order to get ready to sell on Amazon there are a few simple steps. First, you must select a selling plan. Amazon offers two options for this: The Individual selling plan which costs $0.99 per sale, and the Professional selling plan which costs $39.99 per month regardless of how many items you sell. Each plan provides you with a specific group of optional programs.

More features, such as adding multiple users, creating promotions and coupons, listing and managing products in bulk, setting dynamic prices, using Amazon Ads, getting paid in your local currency, and some shipping options are only available to those with the Professional selling plan. In the end, you get to control the cost of selling with Amazon by picking the tools, programs, and services that are right for you as an individual or your business.

Million $ Tip

Amazon also charges referral fees for each sale. These fees vary by product category. For every item sold, you'll pay a percentage of the total price or a minimum amount (usually $0.30), whichever is greater. You might end up paying additional fees for specific services like closing fees, rental book service fees, and high- volume listing fees, as well.

Once you have decided which selling plan to go with, the next step will be setting up a Seller Central account. After choosing your plan, you will register with Amazon using the email address associated with your customer account. You can also create a separate business email address for this. To set up the Seller Central account you will need your bank account and routing numbers, a credit card that can be charged internationally, a government-issued ID, tax information, and a phone number. Once you have access to the Seller Central account you can use it to list and price products, manage inventory, and fulfill orders. You can also use tools in Seller Central to create coupons and promotions, track payments and expenses, and tons more. There is also a free app you can put on your phone to help you keep track of everything.

Additionally, if you are the rights owner for an eligible

brand, you can enroll your brand in the Amazon Brand Registry program before you list your products. This makes it easy to associate your products with your brand name. This service is free and provides sellers with additional selling benefits and tools.

With Amazon, you can choose to fulfill orders yourself, or you can send your inventory to Amazon and have them pick, pack, and deliver products through their fulfillment service. One of the major pluses of letting Amazon handle your products is that they also handle any customer service and returns. The downside to letting Amazon fulfill your products is the extra fees associated with doing so. You will end up incurring a fulfillment cost (based on weight and product category), inventory storage cost, and returns processing fees. My tip to you would be to add up all your costs for fulfilling your own products, then use the **Amazon Revenue Calculator** (sellercentral.amazon.com/hz/fba/profitabilitycalculator/index?lang=en_US) to estimate costs, calculate fees, and find out if you can save using Amazon's fulfillment service.

Amazon has its own payment processing system that it utilizes to pay sellers on its platform. This system records purchases, collects payments, and then holds the funds for a period of time before paying them out. This time period depends on which selling plan you went with. For the Individual selling plan, sellers get paid out every week. The Professional selling plan pays sellers bi-weekly or every 14 days. When you end up with a positive balance, you will get paid out via ACH transfer or electronic funds delivery. If you have a negative balance, it will automatically be deducted from the credit card you have on file.

Although setting up an Amazon Seller Central account

is a little bit more involved than the other resources I have talked about in this chapter, it remains one of the best places to sell large amounts of items.

Pro Tip

When dealing with anyone from Facebook Marketplace, Craigslist, or any other online sales platform, make sure you are thinking about safety first!

You do not want to go to these deals alone. Furthermore, it is best to meet in a well-lit, public setting. You want to make absolutely sure that you are putting your safety and well-being first. Lastly, beware of other scams that may pop up as you post your items. One I experienced recently was a scam where someone tried to get you to verify your phone number by asking for a code. They then use this code to verify your information so they can then use it to mask their own when they make scam calls.

> **Million $ Tip**
>
> You can use scam detection apps to sniff out a well-planned scam. **Norton Genie** is a powerful app that allows you to upload a suspicious screenshot or copy and paste a questionable message. From there, an AI scans it and lets you know how likely it is that the post or message is a scam. Using an app like this can help you make a more informed decision.

Go Forth and Sell!

With the information provided to you in this chapter, you now have the necessary tools to launch your own grand treasure hunt. The rewards are too numerous to mention, and the riches you can make are only limited by the strength of your desire to succeed. Think big, and in no time at all you will be on your way to becoming a Garage Sale Millionaire!

CHAPTER 6

eBay: Virtually Limitless Potential
Buy & Sell Collectibles for Great Money

For any potential Garage Sale Millionaire, one realm rises above all others for making amazing amounts of money. It's an arena where almost any object— baseball cards, toys, action figures, sports memorabilia, art, antiques, watches, DVDs, magazines and books, sporting goods, home and garden items, movie memorabilia, electronics, and even cars—can easily be sought out and acquired, then flipped and sold for sizable profits. That province, conveniently located on the internet, is known as **eBay** (www.ebay.com).

By the time you've finished this chapter, you'll see that eBay is a dynamic, multifaceted online community where almost anything can—and will be—auctioned off to an extremely active and loyal customer base.

Never before in the long history of collecting and treasure hunting has there been one resource that can bring together so many people with so many diverse interests the way that eBay does. eBay has been described as the world's largest garage sale. The reason eBay has continued its momentous growth in popularity lies in the website's simple format, which makes it extremely easy to conduct business. When you want to become a Garage Sale Millionaire, time is money. Selling items on eBay offers maximum simplicity. We all know that time saved equals substantial profits made.

An officer's sword from the Civil War successfully purchased on eBay.

In this chapter, you'll learn many valuable insider tips, gleaned from my own years of experience working on eBay, that will allow you to amplify your quest to make money quickly. These are personal tips that you will absolutely not be able to find anywhere else. My main objective within this chapter is to show you how to make your eBay experience not only more gratifying and fulfilling but exponentially more profitable.

The eBay Homepage—
A Starting Point for Your Garage Sale Millionaire Treasure Hunt

eBay's homepage is divided into ten primary sections:

- **The Top Header**—This is the uppermost section of the eBay homepage, which includes links to sign in or register for a new (and of course, free) account. Also included in the top header section are links to buying and selling items, a link to your personal "My eBay" page—where you will be able to monitor all the auctions you're involved in, a "Contact Us" link to approach eBay directly, a drop-down menu for over thirty different auction categories, links to their Motors and Stores sections, and a link to eBay's Security and Resolution Center.

- **eBay Website Advertising**—eBay lists promotional advertising in this space. Sometimes, links to the Daily Deal—great items to buy and items with deep discounts—will be located here.

- **Daily Deals/Today's Deals**—This section of the homepage includes items eBay highlights for its bidders.

- **My Recent Activities**—Whatever you have

searched for recently on eBay is listed here.

- **Favorite Categories**—Links to over 35 categories of goods and services within the eBay website, as well as a Visit All Categories link.

- **More Fun Finds**—This section highlights additional areas to visit. Some of the items here can include promotional items from television show-sponsored auctions (e.g., Ellen/Oprah) or items for upcoming holidays (e.g., Mother's Day).

- **From Our Sellers**—This section highlights featured items up for auction throughout the website.

- **The Lower Tier**—The bottom of eBays homepage which contains links to many websites within the eBay system. This last section at the bottom of the homepage includes links to all 47 international eBay websites from eBay Argentina to eBay Venezuela; links to more than 15 additional eBay services such as Feedback Forum, Security Center, eBay Returns, Gift Cards & Gift Certificates, and Announcements.

Note that eBay's website content and organization change frequently. The eBay homepage may be altered due to seasonal changes, such as advertising for holidays like Christmas, Chanukah, Easter, and so on, or to promote a special addition to the website.

Searching the Website

Searching for buried treasure is a simple and easy process on eBay. All you have to do is enter what you're looking for in the search criteria dialog box, and then the results of your search will be listed on your computer screen.

The best way to get the most usable hits when you search for items on eBay is to be as detailed as possible. If you use a set of more generic search terms, your search may not yield as many usable results as you would like.

Million $ Tip

When searching for an item on eBay, try searching for it using common misspellings. Some listings may have typos in the title, which means fewer people will find and bid on the item you're interested in. Less bidding competition means you can potentially get your item at a lower price.

If, after your basic search results are displayed, you want to further refine your search criteria, you can do so by finding the "refine search" box on the left side of the page. More categories and empty data fields will be listed here. Another way to refine your search is to check the search, including the title and description box, and then re-type your original search terms.

Hopefully, what will be displayed will be the exact item you're looking for. Information such as featured items (the actual auction item and description), price (the current high bid in the auction), and time left (time remaining in the auction) will be displayed next to a picture of the item for auction. Sometimes, "Free Shipping" or a label of "Top Rated Seller" (for those sellers who meet certain successful sales criteria) will be listed for each sales entry to try to entice you to further investigate a particular auction.

All the pertinent auction information will be displayed for you on this page. Now it's up to you to either investigate a particular auction further or to keep on searching for the exact item you're interested in.

Before You Bid: Understanding the Auction Page

After finding an item you'd like to bid on, you'll need to click on the picture or description to select the item. The auction page you see displayed will have everything you need to make an informed decision on whether or not to bid. It's on this page where your decision to either bid on an item or to look for other items, will be made.

The auction page is split into two sections. The top half of the page gives bidders exact data about the current auction, as well as the seller; the bottom half of the page gives more detailed information about the auction item and details regarding the auction process.

The top half of the eBay auction page displays for the bidder:

Item Condition—Is the item you are interested in new, used, never opened, refurbished, or mint-in-box? You'll find that information here.

Time Left—The time remaining in the auction.

If the auction is getting close to ending, the time left will countdown second-by-second directly on your screen.

Bid History—This shows how many bids have been made so far in this particular auction.

Current Bid—Shows the current price or current highest bid on the item.

Max Bid Field—If the auction is still open, you can place your bid here.

Sale Info—Shipping, payment, and return information will be located under the bid field.

Seller Info—The seller ID, a link to their feedback

profile, feedback percentage, and a link to ask the seller a question will be listed on the right-hand side of the auction page.

The bottom half of the eBay auction page contains more information including:

Description—More specific details, including brand, special features, and dimensions, are listed in this section.

Shipping and Payment Info—This section lists the terms and conditions of the sale, such as shipping costs, estimated delivery time, and any return policies.

More from This Seller—Many times a seller will have multiple auctions on eBay. This section gives you specific hyperlinks to access the auctions for those items.

You might see another option where the current bid price of the auction is listed as "Buy It Now". When this option is available, any bidder can pay the "Buy It Now" price and immediately win the auction item without having to go through the sometimes lengthy auction process. The "Buy It Now" option, when it's offered, is always available if no one has yet placed a bid on an auction. Once the first bid is made, the "Buy It Now" option disappears.

You need to be extra cautious when you are deciding whether or not to place a bid on an item. Because you are not personally familiar with the seller, care must be

> **Million $ Tip**
>
> Not all auctions have a "Buy It Now" option. It is up to the seller to list this option on an auction item. However, you can still contact the buyer to see if they will take your offer and end the auction early.

taken to make sure that the item you want to bid on is exactly what you are interested in buying.

Never bid early on an item. The best time to bid on an item is the final two minutes of any auction. The best and most efficient way to do this is to use sniperware. I will discuss sniperware in more detail later in the chapter.

Getting to Know the Seller

Some great tidbits of information can clue the bidder into whether or not the seller can be trusted, and if he or she is legitimate. You need to carefully examine the "Seller Info" section before you bid on any item. This information is located on the right-hand side of every eBay auction page. The seller info section details valuable information regarding the legitimacy of the seller, including:

The Seller's name—This is the eBay user ID for the seller.

The eBay Seller's Star Rating—This rating denotes positive feedback for the seller participating in this auction. Obviously, the higher the star rating, the more you will trust this person and want to do business with them.

Positive Feedback Percentage—This section shows positive feedback from all past bidders, listed as a percentage. There is also a hyperlink included, which will direct you to the seller's detailed Feedback Profile. Anything under 95% is not good.

Ask a Question—Click this hyperlink if you need to ask the seller anything about the auction.

Save This Seller—You can add the seller to your list of Favorite Sellers and Stores on your personal eBay homepage for quick reference.

Items for Sale or Visit Store—If the seller has other items listed on eBay, you'll be able to quickly access those auctions from here.

Million $ Tip

When an item is first posted to eBay, always check with the seller to see if they will take less than the asking price. You have a better chance of scoring a great deal if the item is being sold by a person who maintains an eBay store, and not one individual selling one individual item.

Protecting Yourself as a Bidder

Properly evaluating the legitimacy of a seller is one of the foremost ways you can protect yourself as a bidder on eBay. There are a few things you can look for when examining the authenticity of a seller.

Study the Seller's Feedback Score and Feedback Percentage. The higher the number score and percentage, the better the odds that a transaction from the seller will be legitimate. You can view this data by clicking on the seller's name directly under the seller info header. Go to

---

Million $ Tip

Be wary of spoof emails from seemingly legitimate sources, such as eBay and PayPal, asking for your financial information. A spoof email is designed to convince the recipient that it is from a trusted sender. Instead, it comes from a criminal source, in an attempt to trick the recipient into unknowingly releasing sensitive personal information, opening up the victim to identity theft.

---

the "Ask a Question" link to ask the seller a question about the item, or to request more information about the item up for auction. Pay careful attention to how quickly the seller answers your questions, and how thorough their responses are. See if the seller offers any additional information about the item.

View all available pictures of the item. Every seller is different and may list this feature in different areas of their eBay auction website. If you don't see a picture listed on the seller's page or the pictures posted to the auction website are not to your liking, email the seller. Ask to see additional photos or evidence that the item is legitimate and to your liking before you make a bid.

Under the Seller's Profile, click the "See All Feedback" hyperlink to see what other users think of this seller's business practices. A more detailed breakdown of the seller's score will be listed here as well, along with the seller's feedback score and feedback percentage.

Million $ Tip

Read the item description very carefully. Never hesitate to ask for more photos and information if you are unsure about the quality, authenticity, or legitimacy of the item you are considering. Always email the seller for clarification. It is better to know all the facts up-front before bidding on something. If they don't answer your email to your liking, do not bid on the item. The last thing you want to do is pay for some- thing that is not exactly as advertised. If the price seems too good to be true, be very careful.

The higher the numbers for a seller, in both the total number of positive responses and feedback percentage, the better. It's much easier to trust someone with 3,500 same is true of feedback in percentage form. If a seller rates 99.0% to 100.0% in positive feedback, potential buyers can be assured that the seller is trustworthy. Also, by clicking on the actual score the seller has received, you get a twelve-month breakdown in one-month, six-month, and twelve-month increments of all sales activity rated as positive, negative, or neutral. This hyperlink will be listed (the seller's score and star icon) directly to the right of the eBay user's ID.

Personal feedback from auction winners is another major plus in verifying the seller's reliability. Of course, anyone on eBay can claim their sale item is the most beautiful of its kind in the world, but a seller's less-than-stellar reputation should make you think twice about bidding on it.

eBay's Buyer Protection Programs

If you don't get what you paid for after the auction is concluded and you've sent your money to the seller, there are certain avenues you can pursue to get some, if not all, of your money back. eBay's buyer protection programs help you with what eBay calls "transactional problems" between a buyer and a seller. However, eBay also wants you to be proactive and try to solve your auction disputes on your own.

If you feel you've been cheated by a seller, eBay prefers you do most of the work yourself before you file a claim. If eBay handled every claim from millions of users around the world, website and company costs would rise exponentially. Always keep the packaging until the dispute is over. If you throw away the packaging, you may not win your claim.

Million $ Tip

You can only get a limited number of negative reviews before you get your eBay selling rights suspended.

A few of the steps you can take before contacting eBay include emailing the seller with questions about the situation, contacting the seller directly by telephone to try to solve a dispute (if a telephone number was given after the auction ended), and contacting your credit card company. Only after the proper steps are followed can you file any protection claim with eBay and access their buyer protection programs. Any claim of this type may take up to 60 days or more after an auction ends before a decision is made about your dispute. Detailed information on this topic can be found on **eBay's Help Page** (ebay.com/help).

In the event of a dispute, you'll need to keep a detailed record of your efforts to resolve it; eBay will require documentation proving what steps were taken before you filed a claim with them. It's not instant gratification but, if you follow the rules, you will eventually get some help. The eBay buyer protection programs range from assistance facilitating communication between buyer and seller to getting reimbursement up to $20,000, with a buyer co-payment of $500, when a vehicle is involved.

Bidding on eBay

Bidding for items on eBay mimics many of the practices and protocols found at a traditional auction house. The usual acts of bidding and re-bidding are the same, and User ratings are similar to popularity contests. When you have a higher user rating as a buyer or seller, more people want to do business with you and, in turn, you become much more popular. As a buyer, being more popular means more sellers will sell to you with fewer or no restrictions. As a seller, being more popular on eBay means more bidders will be attracted to your auctions because you're considered a legitimate and trustworthy vendor.

The complete opposite occurs when your user rating is low. As a seller, not many people will take your auctions seriously. They will view your business dealings as untrustworthy because of your low rating. As a bidder, many sellers won't vend with you because you have proven yourself to be unreliable.

Being Outbid—AKA, Let the Bidding Wars Begin!

After you've placed your bid on an item, you might be outbid. That is usually the rule and not the exception. eBay will issue an automated email reminder stating that you have, in fact, been outbid, with a link back to the auction page so you can try to outbid the higher bidder— or, as I like to say, your competition. If you're like me, you really hate to be outbid in any auction. Losing an auction you know you could have won—losing out on an item you could turn around and sell for a handsome profit—is a very bitter pill to swallow!

Million $ Tip

Sign up to have eBay text your mobile telephone on the status of every auction in which you are involved. Texts will advise you of activity on the item and are helpful if you do not check your email on a regular basis.

Being outbid is not really a problem in the early stages of an auction, because of auto-generated outbid notices. The only time being outbid becomes a serious problem is when you don't check your email often enough. If you can't check your email frequently, you may come to the realization that you're reading an outbid notice for the first time only after the auction you're interested in has already ended. Not good. When this happens, the sting you feel from the loss of an eventual profit lasts for a while.

If you're lucky enough to be the highest bidder when an auction ends, it's now time to pay for the item.

Payment on an Item

After you've won an item, eBay will contact you by email to let you know you were the highest bidder. The email will contain a link, which will take you directly to the payment page for that auction where your credit card will used to pay for that item. Set up your credit card information ahead of time so you don't miss out on paying for something.

> **Million $ Tip**
>
> If you buy more than one item from a seller, ask them to combine shipments to save on the shipping costs.

When you finally receive the item you've won on eBay, make sure you open and inspect it thoroughly within 48 hours so you can report any problems.

After a certain amount of time has transpired, the seller will not feel liable for any problems, and you will be stuck with something defective and non-returnable.

Million $ Tip

Always share your feedback after you receive an auction item. The higher the feedback score you receive as a great buyer, combined with the positive feedback score you give the seller after they deliver an item to you, as promised, helps improve the status you hold in future dealings on eBay.

Sniping and Sniperware: Never Get Outbid on eBay Again

This brings me to snipers and sniperware, and the minute-by-minute of the bidding process. These terms might seem somewhat scary or mysterious, but they describe how individuals, with little or no effort, can swoop in at the very last moment of an online auction and steal the deal you thought you had won. This is even more painful when you realize the item you just lost out on would have made you a substantial profit upon resale.

So, what is sniping? With just moments left to go in an auction or, in many cases, with just one second remaining, someone enters the auction with just barely enough of a bid to outbid you and become the winning bidder. Because of the precise timing of that single, strategically placed bid, so close to the end of the auction, you have no opportunity to counter and save your bid. You are stuck and you have just lost the auction. You are now relegated to dreaming of what could have been.

Congratulations, or rather, my condolences…you have just been sniped by someone using sniperware. The term sniping can also be used to describe someone manually outbidding you at the last moment, without the use of a computer program. However, the term more commonly refers to electronic sniping using software.

In more civilized times, it used to be that the person sniping you would do it manually, physically waiting until the last possible moment to outbid you. This drawn-out process usually meant staying awake until the very end of the auction, to enter and (hopefully) make a winning bid. As a result, you'd become sleep-deprived, despite knowing you had to wake up early the next morning to go to work. However, you waited patiently until the last conceivable moment in your attempt to try and win the auction item. Today, these snipers use technology, in the form of computer programs called sniperware, to do all their dirty bidding work and outmaneuver the non-sniperware-using public.

Unfortunately, you need to arm yourself with sniperware before doing any serious bidding on eBay just to level the playing field. Sniperware can be found and downloaded from the internet as shareware, or software programs that cost the user a fee after a short trial period. I would personally recommend **Auction Defender** (www.auctiondefender.com) or **JustSnipe** (www.justsnipe.com), but a quick internet search will yield countless options.

Creating a Seller's Account and Understanding How to Sell Your Items for a Profit on eBay

Creating Your Account

The first step you must take to become an eBay seller is to

create a Seller's Account. You do this, of course, by filling out yet another online form.

Although there are differences in registering as a seller compared to a buyer, these differences are minor. Once you have registered as a seller on eBay, you can begin the process of listing your items on the website.

Understanding the Different Types of Listings on eBay, and What These Levels Mean for Your Costs and Eventual Profits

Before you get ready to list your items for sale on eBay, or even begin considering how you're going to describe your items to get the best response, you must first understand the different types of listings eBay offers. There are two different types of listings on eBay: Auction and fixed price Buy It Now listings (see table, page 189). Each category offers distinct positives and negatives to the seller.

With a Buy It Now listing, you are allowed to buy or sell items instantly at a set price, just like the "Buy it Now" option within an auction-style listing. This style of listing is most appropriate for sellers that have large quantities of fixed-price items that they need to move, or items that hold a commercial value that is easy to identify and label. The major benefit of using a Buy It Now listing is that you will get better placement on search results, within eBay or on search engines like Google. This translates into a better opportunity to make more substantial profits.

By choosing to sell your items in a fixed-price listing, you can also use the "Best Offer" option to enhance your selling chances. "Best Offer" gives buyers a chance to approach the seller with a direct offer to buy a listed item at a different price than listed, which the seller can choose to accept or decline. The fees for this style of listing can become more expensive than an auction-style listing, depending on the number of items you are listing and the value at which they are listed, as the fees are due per item sold, at the value at which they sold.

Fixed-price listings are only available to sellers who meet certain criteria. To be able to list single-quantity fixed-price items, you must have a feedback rating of 10 or more. To list multiple items in a single fixed-price listing, you must be a registered member for at least 14 days and have a feedback rating of 30 or more.

With an auction-style listing, you are offering an item up to the highest bidder for a duration of 1, 3, 5, 7, or 10 days, with the option to add on a "Buy it Now" price if there isn't much action on the bidding front. This style of listing is most appropriate for sellers with items that are rare, obscure, or difficult to label and appraise. In an eBay auction, your potential buyers determine the value for you, as opposed to you giving it a set value. The two major drawbacks of an auction-style listing are 1) you can only list one item per auction, and 2) you are subject to more fees than a fixed-price listing. Mastering this basic style of eBay listing is vital to your success as a Garage Sale Millionaire.

Listing	Costs	Positives	Negatives
Fixed Price	• Listing fee is based on the total value of the items you list for sale. (Total value is the Buy it Now price multiplied by the quantity of items in the listing.) • Final Value Fee due per item sold, based on the final sale price of each item. • Insertion Fee of 35 cents after the free monthly allotment has been met.	• You can sell more than one item at a time. • No additional fee for "Buy it Now" option. •Listings can last up to 30 days and can be auto renewed or cancelled. •Eligible for more free listings per month as an eBay Store Subscriber.	• Creates a ceiling for profits earned. • Can ultimately cost you more in fees than an auction style listing, depending on the quantity and value of items being listed.
Auction Style	• Listing fee based on the starting price of your item. • Final Value Fee based on final sale price of item. • Can set a. Reserve Price with an extra fee. • Insertion Fee of 35 cents after the free monthly allotment has been met.	• When your item sells, eBay will credit you one Insertion Fee. • No profit ceiling. • Allowed to post listings in this format from the beginning. • Can cost you less in fees than a fixed price listing, depending on the value of the item being listed.	• Can only sell one item per listing. • Can't guarantee how much money you will make, as auctions are unpredictable

Other Need-to-Know Criteria Before You Start Thinking About Selling Items on eBay

In speaking with representatives from eBay while researching this book, I unearthed some essential information that all sellers need to know. Some of this information may seem strict or inflexible, but these caveats are put in place to help eBay run like the well-oiled machine it is.

Before eBay will end their scrutiny of you and your selling activities, you will need to meet the following requirements:

- 90 days have passed since your first successful sale
- You have had more than 25 transactions
- Your total sales equal or exceed $250

Until you meet these three criteria, eBay will hold back all proceeds, from every sale, until your buyers receive the items they have purchased from you. eBay does this to ensure you have acted properly and ethically in all your financial dealings.

Another important piece of information concerns brand name items. In the past, eBay had to heavily regulate users selling brand-name items; membership length and quality (determined via feedback scores) were required to meet certain standards before a seller could list brand-name items. Now, eBay has come up with a whole new system, where the intellectual property rights owners regulate the posts by reporting infringement to eBay directly.

This new system is called the Verified Rights Owner Program, or VeRO for short. VeRO allows the owners of various kinds of intellectual property rights, and their authorized representatives, to report to eBay any listings they find that infringe upon their intellectual property rights. Rights owners also fill out a "VeRO Participant Profile" giving sellers a reference for acceptable practices when re-selling a brand name item.

If you're wondering how this applies to you and your listings, know that repeat VeRO violations are subject to a wide range of consequences—from restrictions on what you can sell, all the way up to full suspension from the website. Fees can't always be refunded on reported listings; it depends on the number of violations you've committed in the past and the specific policy you violated. Being knowledgeable about how different companies want their items represented will protect you and your ability to sell.

If you feel a mistake was made in the reporting of your listing, know that the only way a report can be withdrawn is if the rights owner contacts eBay about withdrawing it. eBay policy states that you alone are responsible for starting the communication about the alleged mistake, directly with the rights owner. In the event you made an actual mistake, know that relisting your item is possible as long as your violation was minor, such as using images or text in the description that aren't yours, or misusing a brand name or logo. However, if you were reported for something more severe, such as listing a counterfeit item, relisting will NOT be possible.

Considering the great margin for error here, eBay has offered users a few tips for ensuring your listing is compliant with VeRO policies:

Create your own content for the listing—Write your own text for your item description and take your own photos for the listing. ALWAYS get permission before using any official logos, images, or texts.

Make sure the statements in your listing are accurate—Rights owners may object to listings that contain false or misleading information about their brand name or products.

Use brand names appropriately—You can mention the brand name you're listing and include photos that you have taken, but do NOT suggest that you're an authorized dealer or reseller if you're not.

Review VeRO Participant Profiles created by Intellectual Property Rights Owners—These profiles are vital to figuring out what language is acceptable with specific products, what imagery is or isn't allowed, and so forth.

Following these tips and referencing the VeRO Participant Profiles will ensure that you are reselling your brand name items honestly and legally—which will be essential to your success as a Garage Sale Millionaire!

I have said it before, and I need to stress it again— your feedback score is very important to your success and livelihood on eBay. Due to the overwhelming number of sellers participating on the website, eBay cannot work personally with every seller. They rely heavily on user feedback to make judgments on how well their vendors are conducting business.

Whenever you sell something on eBay, the buyer has the option to fill out a feedback form grading five aspects of their sales experience. Even though all five are important, there are two main ratings you need to consistently get right to perform well as a seller: communication and shipping.

First, communication is the key to a good transaction. To guarantee no problems occur during the selling process, you need to be very professional and open in all your communications with your customers. You need to answer all emails quickly, monitor your auctions closely in case people have questions for you, and send buyers tracking numbers when you ship items. Make sure they always feel taken care of, until the moment they open the box and are satisfied with the item they purchased from you. If you want to take customer service to the highest level, list your email address and telephone number when sending an invoice.

Second, offer free shipping whenever possible. Buyers love free shipping, and offering this relatively low-cost extra goes a long way toward ensuring your customers remain happy customers. Additionally, thanks to eBay's Global Shipping Program, you can now easily ship your sale items internationally by routing them through eBay's domestic shipping center. eBay handles the customs process for you, takes responsibility for lost/damaged items, and protects you against negative feedback. You can still offer your customers free domestic shipping to the shipping center, automatically securing a perfect score on shipping costs. Moreover, by using the Global Shipping Program, you can increase your audience exponentially.

Make communication and shipping your top priority in every transaction, and there is a great chance you will get a perfect score on buyer feedback. As a bonus, making sure the customer comes first and taking care of your customers from the start of any auction will eventually help you secure lower fees on future auctions.

Opening Up Your Store On eBay

The key to being efficient and profitable on eBay is opening a store. This offers the seller significant benefits in the form of discounts, tools that optimize your selling experience, and even a customizable store page.

So how does an up-and-coming Garage Sale Millionaire get this ball rolling? Before you begin setting up a store, be sure that you have an active seller's account that is registered with an automatic payment system. Also, have an idea of what features your store may need. Consider the type of items you sell, how often you sell, and the volume of your sales.

> **Million $ Tip**
>
> If you plan to sell big-ticket items, sell them through your store. eBay will cap how much you have to pay in commission fees per item.

If you're wondering what benefits making a store might hold for you, or if you don't have an idea of what kind of store you need, look no further than this paragraph. Store types are based on the seller's needs, in terms of sales volume and company size. In order of cost, from lowest to highest, the store types are Starter, Basic, Premium, Anchor, and Enterprise. The first two options are best for occasional sellers up to growing small businesses. The last three options are best for companies with a high sales volume and significant support needs, which is why the cost escalates with each level.

> **Million $ Tip**
>
> Name your eBay site your company name. This will increase name recognition with your brand and products.

All store types come with access to promoted listings, the promotions manager, and exclusive tools to perfect your listings, such as automatic renewal every month. Extra goodies include a "Featured

Items" section on your page, which allows you to choose merchandise to display more prominently, as well as store categories, to help you organize all your merchandise for a quality shopping experience.

Now that those considerations have been addressed, it's time to set up your store. Go to "Account" within your "My eBay" page and select "Subscriptions". Then select "Choose a Store". Once you find the type of store that fits your specific needs, click "Select and review". Next, you will select a subscription payment term (yearly or monthly), create a unique name for your store, and finish up with the "Submit order" option to purchase your new store subscription.

Once your name is finalized, eBay will create a website address for your store, offer tips, and provide a lot of help to get your new store up and running. They'll help with everything from personalizing your store, organizing your inventory, and allowing you to preview how it looks to buyers so that you can tweak your page to perfection. With all these new tools at your disposal, your eBay success is almost ensured!

Researching eBay for Better Profits

For the successful Garage Sale Millionaire, doing proper research before marketing and selling your items on eBay means the difference between incremental profits and substantial profits. Along with spending quality time on eBay—looking at what kind of items are listed, how they are listed, who may be buying items, and for what amounts—take a few moments to look at and study the **eBay Seller Center (**<u>www.ebay.com/sh/ovw</u>**)**. This section of the website offers invaluable tips and strategies for how to best use eBay to your ultimate advantage.

The topics at the eBay Seller Center, listed in detailed tutorial form, include:

Get Started—How eBay works, how to register, and how to buy with confidence are just a few of the topics discussed.

Create Listings—How to create listings, pricing guidance, and other tips for first-time eBay sellers.

Manage Listings—Marketing tips, security standards, third-party listing tools, and more.

Promote Listings—Strategies for promoting your items, boosting traffic, and using social media.

Run Your Store—Information concerning eBay Store subscriptions.

Shipping Before Sale—In-depth information on shipping options, calculations, international shipping, and more.

Shipping After Sale—Packing tips, explanations of carriers, and eBay shipping labels.

Great Service—eBay's expectations for customer service, returns, and case resolution, as well as an in-depth explanation of the Top-Rated Program.

Payments & Fees—A complete listing of fee structures, funds availability, tax information, and other money-specific issues.

Additional Resources—Any miscellaneous items that were excluded above, such as eBay community links, announcements, help pages, webinars, and more!

The Benefits of Becoming an eBay Top-Rated Seller

There are sellers on eBay and then there are Top Rated Sellers on eBay. As the name would seem to imply, a Top-Rated Seller is a much better designation.

According to eBay, Top Rated Sellers rank among the most successful sellers on eBay for both sales and customer satisfaction. The Top-Rated Seller icon is placed next prominently on their qualified listings, indicating that the seller meets the following criteria:

- No more than 0.3% of cases closed without seller resolution and two or fewer cases
- A transaction defect rate of .5% or lower with defects from no more than three buyers
- eBay marketplace compliance
- A late shipment rate of 3% or lower and five or fewer late shipments
- A rate of 95% of shipments with uploaded and verified tracking within the indicated handling time
- The seller's eBay account has been active for at least 90 days.

You will also need to have a minimum of 100 transactions (items you've sold and purchases you've made) and have $1,000 in sales with US buyers in the last 12 months in order to apply. If a seller ceases to comply with any of the above requirements, they are removed from the program.

When a bidder sees the Top-Rated Seller icon in any auction, the bidder can be assured they are dealing with someone who has earned a stellar reputation on the website. From eBay's website, the Top-Rated Seller program benefits include:

Enhanced Search Result Visibility — Top Rated Sellers receive enhanced visibility in eBay search results and exclusive seller protections.

Additional Seller Protections — Top Rated Sellers who offer 30-day or longer returns and reside in the US receive additional protection benefits.

Rating Protection and Shipping Credit for False "Item Not as Described" Claims — eBay will credit up to $6 shipping cost per return and will remove any negative feedback from service metrics on false "item not as described" claims.

Partial Refund Deduction on Used or Damaged Returns — To help offset the decreased value of a used or damaged return item, eBay will allow Top Rated Sellers to deduct up to 50% of the refund.

Eligibility for Top Rated Plus Status — Top Rated Sellers who offer handling times of 1 business day or less and a free 30-day return policy can reach Top Rated Plus status.

Prominent Status Seal on Listings (Top Rated Plus) — A Top Rated Plus seal will be prominently displayed on your qualifying listings, letting shoppers know that you are a reputable and trustworthy seller.

Discounted Final Value Fees (Top Rated Plus) — As a Top-Rated Plus Seller, you get 10% off final value fees (with some exclusions).

UPS Rate Discounts— Top Rated Sellers can receive up to a 23% discount on UPS Ground daily rates.

Exclusive Networking— Top Rated Sellers share selling strategies on an exclusive discussion board, open only to Top Rated Seller members.

Special Offers— eBay works with many companies that offer products, services, and discounts available only to Top Rated Sellers.

Understanding and Determining the Value of an Item—The eBay Way

Monetary Cost versus Emotional Value

Many times, emotional value, or the emotional currency someone places on an item, far outweighs the actual cost of an item or its monetary cost. In these instances, the idea of getting the best value or price for an item falls somewhat by the wayside. In an emotional value purchase, the buyer must have that item no matter what—no ifs, ands, or buts!

For example, when I bought a 1:1 scale, life-size Star Wars' Darth Vader action figure, #288 of 500, I spent approximately $6,100 for it (give or take a few cents). I later referenced the 4th Edition of the Star Wars Super Collectors *Wish Book* by Geoffrey T. Carlton, to verify the piece's value and ascertain the wisdom of my investment. I discovered the estimated value of the piece to be only $4,500. The difference in the cost of the item versus the estimated value of the collectible was about $1,600—a substantial amount of money. Was that a bad investment? When considering the numbers…maybe. As it turns out, it was a great investment, on several different levels.

Million $ Tip

As a buyer or seller on eBay, it is essential to know how to evaluate the value of an item so that you can get the best deal (as a buyer) or make the highest profit (as a seller). **Terapeak Product Research** and **Terapeak Sourcing Insights** (www.terapeak.com) are eBay's free Research Tools in the Seller Hub that can help you determine the value of an item, provide market insights, identify trending categories, and even highlight areas that have high search volume but not enough active listings to meet the demand.

The first question I had to ask is, will the piece rise in value over time? The answer is, yes, it probably will. Why? The piece is a limited-edition item with a lower issue number. Moreover, the company that made this collectible no longer produces Darth Vader 1:1 scale replicas. This item was rare, hard to find, and of high overall quality—and I had been feverishly trying to get my hands on it for over a decade.

The emotional value compared to the monetary cost was very high, and the thought of getting the piece solely for monetary gain became secondary. Emotion completely won out over saving money. Would I have spent more money than I eventually paid to acquire this collectible? The answer is probably yes. I happily accepted the offer and gladly paid the $6,100 because of the important emotional currency associated with acquiring the item.

Estimating Value on eBay

So, how does one go about estimating the monetary value of an item on eBay? There are several methods to use.

First, you can search for duplicate items, or items very similar to your items of interest. By studying how others describe similar items, you can describe your items accordingly for profitable auctions. By understanding how much others are bidding for similar items, you can see the real market value—or at least the eBay market value—that buyers are willing to pay. You can also do an advanced search on closed auction items and see how much these items have sold for in the past.

If you are interested in a one-of-a-kind piece, or an item that can't easily be compared to other listings, then you need to use other resources on the internet to your advantage. You should also search bookstores for a collectibles price guide that includes the item you're interested in. This is especially important for a buyer if the bidding or sales price on the item is escalating rapidly. You need to do as much research as possible on the value of the specific item you want to buy, not only to save money when you purchase it but also to make as much money as possible when you sell it.

The time you spend making sure you're not getting ripped off is time well spent. Hopefully, you will come across the auction in its infancy, so you have adequate time to do your research and make an informed decision.

Would I go to great lengths to research something in detail that is being sold or auctioned for a couple of dollars? Probably not. However, as the monetary stakes rise in a high-priced auction, the more informed you are, the better, so you don't pay too much for an item. From the seller's side, the opposite is true. As a true Garage

Sale Millionaire, you can always hope your inexpensive items increase in value, as an uninformed public continues to line your pockets with higher and higher bids.

> ## Million $Tip
>
> The number one time of year to sell any item on eBay is 30 days prior to Christmas.
> What is the second-best time of year to sell on eBay? Right in front of any major holiday, such as Mother's Day, Father's Day, Valentine's Day, etc. January is the worst time of year to sell anything on eBay.

In the end, you are the ultimate judge as to what may be too high a monetary cost for you, or what you may consider a financial steal. Once again, you have to consider monetary cost versus emotional value. Even when you weigh the monetary cost against emotional value, in the end, a dollar is still a dollar. If you've found the true value of an item that piques your interest and you've done the research to determine its value, you're still the one who must make the final decision.

Avoiding Fraud as a Seller

One of the more unfortunate facts about eBay is that the website will never be 100% free of individuals looking to make a quick buck at your expense—people who will take your money for an item that is invalid, misrepresented, or maybe never even existed. With so many individuals making up a global internet community, some evildoers will inevitably lurk about within the system. eBay does an admirable job in policing its website to rid it of unsavory online predators, who seek to defraud users via bogus auctions and fraudulent dealings. However, as diligent as eBay is, they cannot stop everyone who tries to take unfair advantage of honest, unsuspecting bidders.

As a seller, the only real type of fraud you need to be aware of involves incoming payments for sold items. However, if you meet your commitments as a seller on eBay, eBay will protect you if you face events out of your control, abusive buyer behavior, and more according to their policies, transaction monitoring, and a dedicated seller protection team that works around the clock to enforce these policies and catch things before they become a problem.

Sometimes sellers offer to accept payment upon pick-up for an auction item. Payment upon pickup means that the seller may agree to accept alternative payment methods if the buyer picks up the item in person after winning an auction. Other means of payment—such as cashier's checks, money orders, or cash—can only be accepted if the bidder picks up an auction win in this fashion. I highly recommend against this practice, due to the potential fraud issues associated with accepting non-guaranteed funds.

Although stop payments are strictly regulated on cashier's checks or money orders, some banks will still place stop payments on these types of transactions. According to John Burnett of BankersOnline.com,

> A bank may refuse payment of its cashier's check under certain circumstances such as alteration, forged endorsement, or a claim against the payee/presenter. But it should be sure of its position before doing so because the penalties for wrongfully refusing payment are stiff. Particularly when a holder in due course is involved, the bank that refuses payment of its own cashier's check is walking in a minefield. Another situation when a bank may refuse payment

of a cashier's check is in the special circumstance of a lost, stolen, or destroyed check.

Instead of having to deal with this type of potential fraud and financial headache, I believe it is best to always use electronic payment services for your business transactions. Just remember, when you list payment terms in your auction, you must make sure to detail what is considered acceptable payment, and what the specific terms are. That way, you're protected against any misunderstandings that might occur when payment is due.

Listing Your Items on eBay

Considering all the detailed research you've conducted, you now know, with certainty, how to best describe your sale items to distinguish them from the multitudes of listings found on the eBay marketplace. You also know your starting auction price for those items. It's now time to fill in the listing information and get your item some expo- sure so that the eBay world can see your offering and, of course, bid handsomely on it.

> **Million $ Tip**
>
> When selling an item, make sure your auction ends at a proper time during the day to ensure more bidders can bid on your items. The optimal time to end an auction is between 10:00 AM and 7:00 PM, Monday through Friday.

Here are questions you have to consider regarding your item:

Proper category and sub-category—Under what categories will you list your sale items to best describe what you want to sell?

Listing your item in a second or third category—By listing your items in different categories, you will attract more bidders.

Starting bid price—What will the starting price be on your sale items? This is very important because you don't want to undervalue or overvalue your items. If you undervalue the item, you leave money on the table. If you overvalue the item, it does not sell.

Minimum bid you will accept for the item—When you set up your auction, this is the bid you place as the minimum starting bid. The minimum bid is also called the reserve price. You can only use this option if you are signed up for a current- level type of auction on eBay.

Specific item details—Color, size, speed—whatever makes the item you want to sell unique. Be very accurate when describing your sale items. Also, eBay doesn't like it when you use the adjective *like* in your auction descriptions and will remove your item from the website if you do. For example: the Fontana Watch, just *like* a Rolex. Instead try the terms *comparable to, matching,* or even *equivalent*.

What pictures to upload—eBay bidders absolutely love to see detailed pictures of your sale item. If you want to move your sale merchandise quickly, upload some great pictures of what you're trying to sell. Post photos from multiple angles and scales, to best replicate the experience of shopping in a physical store, where buyers can examine objects in person.

The duration of the auction—I recommend an auction length of seven days. By setting up an auction to last a week, you have the best possible opportunity to receive the most traffic, and highest number of unique hits, for your auction.

Terms of the sale—What types of payment will you accept for the sale of your auction items, and what are the relevant details for your auction? The acceptable methods of payment (e.g., PayPal), any additional shipping costs, your return policy, and how long the winning bidder has to pay before he defaults on the auction, must be listed in this section. The clearer you are when listing your auction details means fewer potential problems later down the road.

There are additional options you can choose to feature in your listing, including extra pictures of your item, a border around your listing, or having your item spotlighted in the Featured Area of the search and listings page. These options are not free, but will, in the long run, help your auction stand out that much more.

> **Million $ Tip**
>
> When you get an offer for your item, if it is anywhere close to what you want, accept it. The chances are very good that, if you decline their first offer, they won't make a second.

Managing Your eBay Listing and Completing the Sale

From your personal My eBay page, you can constantly track multiple auctions, and easily check the status of all the auctions in which you are involved in. Your My eBay page is an essential element in becoming a successful seller, especially if you're buying and selling multiple items at the same time.

It functions as a control center, helping you organize and refine your efforts and also see what's selling, what's not selling, and if you are the big winner on any of the items you've been bidding on. The My eBay page also has an abundance of other tools; you can save a list of your favorite sellers, monitor feedback on your eBay activities, view messages sent to you by other bidders and sellers, or generated by eBay, and view announcements from the site as well.

The Last Major Step in the eBay Selling Process is Completing the Sale

When one of your auctions is completed, eBay will autogenerate an email to you stating who the highest bidder was, their shipping address, and the winning bid amount. Because you clearly stipulated payment terms when you originally set up your auction, you may not hear from the high bidder until funds are received from the auction. However, you might still get an email from the buyer asking additional questions about the payment process. This is a normal part of the eBay auction process, even if you have one of the best, most detailed sales pages possible. Reply with the appropriate answers immediately.

Because you took great care, and paid great attention to detail, when posting your auction to the website, all you have to do now is wait for payment from the customer and ship the item. If, for some reason, the buyer delays sending funds for several days, you can follow up with a friendly reminder email about payment.

Always be a great communicator on eBay and your customers will love you! More importantly, they will love the way you do business. eBay is glutted with sellers who are terrible communicators, treat their customers horribly, and make doing business with them a nightmare. A competent, successful sales and businessperson stands out as exceptional. After receiving consistently positive feedback on your customer feedback page, people will more easily respect you and will want to continue to do business with you.

Logging Off eBay

As you explore eBay on your own, you will discover a treasure trove of valuable information at your fingertips just waiting to be discovered. eBay is a relatively simple website to get to know, and it is easy to navigate and browse for hours at a time. With this information, you will be a Garage Sale Millionaire in no time!

CHAPTER 7

How to Assign a Value to Your New Treasures

Properly valuing your new-found treasures is one of the most important aspects of becoming a successful Garage Sale Millionaire. If the items you find during your treasure-hunting endeavors are not valued correctly; you could be short-changing yourself and losing out on a lot of money when you decide to sell.

If you price an item too low, you'll lose out on the money you could have potentially made on the sale. If you price an item too high, you may never be able to make the sale at all. The actual practice of putting a price tag on any item is never an easy one. Even the most knowledgeable experts can sometimes find it difficult to determine the best price for an item. There are two different options available for properly and accurately valuing your treasures. You can complete a self-valuation, or you can pay a professional to do the job for you. No matter which option you choose, you'll have to value your items as accurately as you can in order to make as much money as possible.

A pair of dueling pistols used in the late 1700s. I bought them from a vendor at a gun show. I couldn't get him down to the price I wanted, so I told him we would flip a coin: my price if it's heads, and your price if it's tails. He thought it was such a great way to negotiate that he agreed—and let's just say I got them at a better price.

Self-Valuation Goes High Tech

The only costs associated with self-valuing items are your personal time spent, and perhaps buying a book or two to assist you with the process. However, nowadays, there are hundreds of amazing apps that you can use to value your items. With these amazing new apps, you can literally use your phone to take a picture of your item, and the app will price it and describe it for you. From there you can put it on eBay or another platform to sell it. For example, you can use **CardBase** (www.getcardbase.com) or the **PSA** (www.psacard.com) app for any trading card you have from Baseball to Pokémon and everything in between. Just simply scan the card or manually enter its information, and these apps will pull up not only all the card details but value as well. They will also let you know when cards go up or down in value with real-time notifications. **CoinSnap** or **CoinID** can be used to value coins of any kind. Just like the other apps mentioned here, you simply scan your coin using your phone's camera. **Stamp ID Pro** and **Stamp Identifier** are two good apps for valuing stamps via that same method.

When it comes to vinyl records, **Discogs** (www.discogs.com) and **iCollect Music** are two great apps that both allow you to search a large database of music but also allow you to scan vinyl barcodes to find detailed information and value. To find values for used books, **BookScouter** (www.bookscouter.com) and **PangoBooks** (www.pangobooks.com) are two great apps in which you can use your phone's camera to scan the book's barcode and get information on value. You can sell books directly through these two apps or just use the value information to post your books on eBay. When it comes to comic book value there are several apps out there, but in my opinion, the most ac- curate values come from doing a reverse image search or barcode search on the comic book through eBay's app. The other resource for comic books is **CGC** (www.cgccomics.com) which I go into more explanation about later in this chapter.

When it comes to antique guns, **GunBroker** (www.gunbroker.com) is a fantastic website to find information and value on new and old guns and ammo.

For toys, eBay seems to be the best place to go. There are several websites out there that can help you, such as **ToyMart Price Guide (**www.toymart.com**),** but these are often specific to certain brands of toys.

A key aspect of determining an item's physical condition and potential resale value is called grading. As we work our way through this chapter, I will discuss grading in more detail. I will also cover the top collectibles to buy and sell so you can increase your profits.

eBay

Although eBay was covered extensively in the previous chapter, I want to reinforce the importance of using this invaluable internet community as an efficient and accurate resource for determining the proper market value of items you're looking to buy and sell.

When buying and selling collectibles on eBay, the idea of market value plays a prominent role. Market value refers to the dollar amount people are willing to pay for an item. Every item listed on eBay, as well as every bid made on those items, helps to continuously reset the current market value. For example, if an original 1984 edition of an Optimus Prime Transformers collectible toy is put up for auction for $1,600, then that becomes the current market value for that collectible. The market value of an item is affected if people continue to place higher bids on that item. The new current market value is established based on the actual selling price. Any subsequent listing of this collectible toy will similarly be priced at, or very close to, that final sales price.

In Chapter 6, I mentioned the fact that many individuals regard eBay as the world's largest garage sale. Now, I would like to take that concept a step further. I also believe that eBay should be considered the world's largest pricing guide. I'd venture to bet not many people think of eBay along those lines. Although they're a fabulous resource to have, the obvious problem with price guides in book form is that once the word is printed on the page that price is finite. The stated market value of items is locked in when that book comes off the printing press for publication. eBay is the best price guide available because it evolves minute-by-minute. Every time an item is listed, bid on, and sold; eBay becomes a newly updated price guide.

To verify what items have sold for at past auctions on eBay requires a little digging, accomplished by performing an advanced search. On eBay's homepage, click the "Advanced" link directly to the right of the main item search box. You'll be redirected to a secondary search page.

About a quarter of the way down the page you will find a "Completed Items" box. Check the box and then re-submit the search criteria you originally entered on the previous page. After you've submitted your search criteria, all the completed auctions that contain the item you are looking for will be displayed on the screen in front of you. You can also find the "Completed Items" box in the left sidebar after you submit a search, just scroll down to the "Show Only" section and select "Completed Items".

One of the newest features on eBay is the **Product Research** (formerly known as Terapeak) option. Here you can look at items that have sold anytime up to three years in the past. You'll go to the Seller Hub, and go to the Research tab. On mobile, head to the Selling tab and then scroll down to Product Research. Depending on how popular an item is, there could be hundreds of pages, and thousands of search results to look through before you're able to find an item that interests you. This service provides access to years of sales data for millions of items, allowing you to analyze trends, competition, and best-selling products. With Product Research, you can research average prices, sell-through rates, shipping costs, and more to help you optimize your listings and pricing strategy for success on eBay. This feature simply requires an eBay store subscription.

WorthPoint

Another invaluable resource for valuing your treasures is **WorthPoint** (www.worthpoint.com). Experts contributing to the website are called Worthologists and bring decades of experience to the site. Worthpoint.com also houses one of the world's largest collecting databases. You can connect with other collectors interested in buying, selling, or swapping stories, and share your insight and knowledge through their forums.

After a free trial period, full access to the website is only available through a paid membership. Membership is offered on three levels: Price Guide Premium, Marks

& Library, and All Access. Some membership benefits include access to extensive valuation data, a collecting community of over 400,000 members, and access to a wealth of information and data about collecting.

Google

Another avenue to navigate when valuing your collectibles is a site you're probably familiar with: **Google** (www.google.com). With any search on Google, there is an upside and a downside. The good news is that you will probably be able to find an extensive list of websites that deal in specific genres of collectibles. The bad news is it may take a substantial time investment to search through all those hundreds, thousands, and sometimes even millions of search results to find the specific information in which you were interested.

For example, try conducting a basic Google search for Barbie dolls. I entered this basic search string recently, and approximately 10,700,000 search results came back including pretty much everything under the sun and then some regarding Barbie dolls. Results included the official website for Mattel, the company that makes the dolls, some websites covering the detailed history of Barbie dolls, a multitude of websites dedicated to methods for collecting the dolls, numerous enthusiast websites for showing off pictures of doll collections, various listings for dolls like Bratz, which are similar to Barbie dolls, and several retail toy websites that just sell them. This is a lot of information to sift through. When you enter more detailed search criteria, as in "Barbie Dolls + 1965 + Redhead," only 335,000 results are retrieved. This is more pertinent information which, as a result, will help you find more accurate valuation data.

Million $ Tip

For collectibles that are not so common, you will need to put in a little more effort to find the value. When you find a website that sells your item, make sure you compare size, color, and any markings that are on the collectible. Give the owner of the website a call and compare your item to theirs. There is a good chance they may have an interest in your treasure, and you will have a fantastic sales opportunity! If an offer is made, I recommend comparing the potential value of your item with a few other vendors before you accept. You might also check to see if the same item is being sold for more somewhere else on the internet.

By making your Google search criteria more detailed, you will have the best success in finding specific data that best suits your needs.

Blogs, News Sites, and Community Forums

After you've identified websites that have the information you need to value your items for eventual sale, delve a little bit deeper into each website. Many of them will also have blogs, news sites, or community forums available for you to read and gather more information about your area of interest. There may also be links to other websites with even more links for you to investigate, containing essential reading material that could give you more insight into your items, and the best opportunity to make valuable sales. Everything you learn from these resources will help shape your ideas and opinions on how to properly value your items.

Using Professionals: Appraisers and Professional Grading Services

Appraisers

Hiring an experienced appraiser is one of the most accurate ways to determine current—and potential—market value for your collectibles. Depending upon an appraiser's level of experience, you could gain tremendous insight from their knowledge of current and anticipated selling trends. This information can certainly be used to your advantage when either selling an item or negotiating a price with a customer. Appraisers can be found in almost every city. How good they are in their ability to properly and accurately appraise items is another question altogether.

It's incumbent upon you to verify the credentials for a quality appraisal service. You can do this via telephone, in person, and online. Check to see if the appraisal company you are interested in is certified by a national or international appraisal agency. **The American Society of Appraisers** (www.appraisers.org) is one of the better-known national certifying appraisal agencies and organizations. Also check to see if the appraiser is endorsed by the **Better Business Bureau** (www.bbb.org), and whether or not there are complaints filed against them.

Coins

There are many coin-grading services available to the treasure hunter trying to determine the quality or condition of their coins. Grading fees typically start at $10 for each coin and can increase from there. Once a coin is grad- ed, the professional coin-grading service that graded your item will enclose your graded coin in a certified and sealed coin holder that not only protects your newly graded coin but also displays pertinent data about your coin and its respective grade. This data includes the year the coin was minted, the denomination of the coin, the actual grade of the coin, and a bar code. The bar code is imprinted on the outside of the protective casing by the grading company, in case they need to reference the coin at some future date.

The condition and grading of a coin play a major role in determining its eventual resale value. According to the Professional Coin Grading Service website, the condition of a coin is defined as "the state of preservation of a particular numismatic issue," and grade is defined as "the numerical or adjectival condition of a coin." Professional coin-grading services use letter and numerical designations to show what they believe is a coin's most accurate grade. The numerical scale used by these grading companies is a 70-point scale that designates the incremental quality of each coin. The more pristine the coin's condition, the higher the numerical grade will be. Letter designations are just as important as the numerical score. Each letter designation relates to the overall quality of the coin as well.

One of the best coin-grading services available to the collector is the **Professional Coin Grading Service (PCGS)** (www.pcgs.com). Most of the industry grades coins according to the PCGS grading system. Notice the following grading charts from the PCGS website. The first chart (page 209) displays a particular coin grade and a description of what each grade means. The second chart (page 210) explains each letter grade in the first chart.

Grade	Description
PO-1	Identifiable date and type.
FR-2	Mostly worn, though some detail is visible
AG-3	Worn rims but most lettering is readable though worn.
G-4	Slightly worn rims, flat detail, peripheral lettering nearly full
G-6	Rims complete with flat detail, peripheral lettering full.
VG-8	Design worn with slight detail.
VG-10	Design worn with slight detail, slightly clearer
F-12	Some deeply recessed areas with detail, all lettering sharp.
F-15	Slightly more detail in the recessed areas, all lettering sharp.
VF-20	Some definition of detail, all lettering full and sharp.
VF-25	Slightly more definition in the detail and lettering.
VF-30	Almost complete detail with flat areas.
VF-35	Detail is complete but worn with high points flat.
EF-40	Detail is complete with most high points slightly flat.
EF-45	Detail is complete with some high points flat.
AU-50	Full detail with friction over most of the surface, slight flatness on high points.
AU-53	Full detail with friction over % or more of the surface, very slight flatness on high points.
AU-55	Full detail with friction on less than % of the surface, mainly on high points.
AU-58	Full detail with only slight friction on the high points.
MS/PR-60	No wear. May have many heavy marks/hairlines, strike may not be full.
MS/PR-61	No wear. Multiple heavy marks/hairlines, strike may not be full.
MS/PR-62	No wear. Slightly less marks/hairlines, strike may not be full.
MS/PR-63	Moderate number/size marks/hairlines, strike may not be full.
MS/PR-64	Few marks/hairlines or a couple of severe ones, strike should be average or above.
MS/PR-65	Minor marks/hairlines though none in focal areas, above average strike.
MS/PR-66	Few minor marks/hairlines not in focal areas, good strike.
MS/PR-67	Virtually as struck with minor imperfections, very well struck.
MS/PR-68	Virtually as struck with slight imperfections, slightest weakness of strike allowed.
MS/PR-69	Virtually as struck with minuscule imperfections, near full strike necessary.
MS/PR-70	As struck, with full strike.

The condition and subsequent grade of a coin, and how these qualities equate to market and potential resale value, can be explained in the following example. Let's say you owned two 1893-CC Morgan Dollars. Both coins look the same, although one is a bit more worn than the other.

They have the same design, have the same mintmark, and both are dated 1893. After getting the coins graded, you realize that one of your 1893 Morgan Dollars was graded as an EF-40 and the other was graded as an MS/PR-67. The difference in grade seems minor at first.

Is the difference between an EF-40 (extra fine condition) grade compared to an MS/PR-67 (mint strike/proof condition) grade that important? Yes! According to the **PCGS Price Guide** (www.pcgs.com/prices), an EF-40 graded 1893-S Morgan Dollar is valued at $8,750 as of August 2018, whereas an MS/PR-67 1893-S Morgan Dollar is valued at $1,200,000.

Grade	Description
PO	Poor
FR	Fair
AG	About Good
G	Good
VG	Very Good
F	Fine
VF	Very Fine
EF	Extremely Fine
AU	About Uncirculated
MS	Mint State
PR	Proof

The nuances in the quality and condition of coins and their subsequent grades, based on specific criteria, can affect the value of every coin. By using a professional coin grading service, the potential of inaccurately grading valuable coins will be avoided.

Comic Books

Certified Guaranty Corporation Comics (CGC Comics) (www.cgccomics.com) is the only professional grading company available for comics and comic books. Fees start in the $25+ range for grading one comic and can escalate to hundreds of dollars if multiple comics or comic books are submitted. The success of CGC Comics comes from their attention to detail and their thoroughness throughout all facets of the comic book grading process. Their four-step process in the valuing of comic books involves receiving (getting the comic book shipped from the customer), grading (judging the physical condition of the comic book and assigning a grade), encapsulation (placing the comic in a protective sleeve or casing) and shipping (sending the comic book back to the customer).

The industry standard for grading comic books is based on the 0.5--- 10.0 CGC Comics Scale. A grade of 0.5 is the lowest score a comic can receive, and it is an example of a comic of poor quality. A grade of 10.0 is the best grade score a comic can possibly achieve and denotes that this collectible is in the best possible, or gem mint, condition. The CGC Scale is as follows:

Grade	Condition	Grade	Condition
0.5	Poor	6.0	Fine
1.0	Fair	6.5	Fine +
1.5	Fair/Good	7.0	Fine/Very Fine
1.8	Good	7.5	Very Fine -
2.0	Good	8.0	Very Fine

2.5	Good +	8.5	Very Fine +
3.0	Good/Very Good	9.0	Very Fine/Near Mint
3.5	Very Good -	9.4	Near Mint
4.0	Very Good	9.6	Near Mint +
4.5	Very Good +	9.8	Near Mint/Mint
5.0	Very Good/Fine	9.9	Mint
5.5	Fine -	10	Gem Mint

Top comic books, when properly graded by a professional grading company, can be valued at more than $1 million. You can view current listings of the top-valued comic books, coins, and magazines at **Nostomania** (www.nostomania.com) Comic book values, like the values from any type of collectible, are always in a state of flux. The chart showing the values of the top 100 comic books is just a snapshot of a particular comic book's value on a particular day.

I bought this Iron Man #1 in fine to very good condition at one of the first garage sales I attended almost 50 years ago, for roughly fifty cents. It is now worth between $200 and $1000+ depending on where you look and its condition. Mine now has a rip on the cover and after sending it in to be graded, it came back as a 4.5 Very Good +. Even though this grade could be considered low, the comic book is still rare enough that I can still sell the piece for around $550 (and that's on the low end for that particular grade!). Not a bad investment when you're only nine years old!

Action Figures

Action Figure Authority (AFA) (www.cgagrading.com/afa/) is the only professional grading service available for action figures. AFA uses three very detailed grading scales to accurately grade action figures: the C-Scale (Condition Scale), the AFA 3-Tier Grading Scale (for items produced from 1995 to present), and the AFAM (M for "modern") 3-Tier Grading Scale (for items produced from 1995 to pre- sent).

As with all grading scales in the collectibles market, a higher score equates to a higher assigned value. A higher value means that higher potential profits can be made. The three AFA grading scales are:

1) C-Scale (Condition Scale)

Grade	Condition
CI-C4	Very poor, badly damaged, basically only useful for spare parts.
C5	Poor condition with heavy wear, broken parts will impair function.
C6	Fair, significant wear, may have some broken parts.
C7	Good, noticeable wear but no broken parts, items may be missing accessories.
C8	Very good, some minor wear, no broken or missing parts.
C9	Near mint condition, very minor imperfections apparent.
C10	Mint condition, unused.

2) AFA 3-Tier Grading Scale (for items produced from 1995 to present)

Grade	Condition
AFA Gold	Gem Mint (100), Mint (95) and Near Mint/Mint (90)
AFA Silver	Near Mint Plus (85), Near Mint (80) and Excellent Plus/ Near Mint (75)
AFA Bronze	Excellent Plus (70), Excellent (60), Very Good (50), Good (40), Fair (30), Poor (20) and Very Poor (10)

3) AFAM 3-Tier Grading Scale (for items produced from 1995 to present)

Grade	Condition
AFAM Gold	9.0, 9.25, 9.5, 9.75 and 10.0
AFAM Silver	7.5, 8.0 and 8.5
AFAM Bronze	1.0-7.0

As a Garage Sale Millionaire, leaving grading judgments to the professionals regarding action figures is one of the best decisions you can make. Because there are so many variables that can determine the condition of your action figure, it's really best to leave grading decisions to the experts. Having the proper grade on an action figure collectible is key to making the most money possible from every sale.

Baseball Cards, Sports Trading Cards, and Non-Sports Trading Cards

Consider the following: there are 30 professional Major League Baseball teams playing every year, every team's roster is made up of 40 players, many players get called up from the minor leagues every year to the big leagues, the sport has been played professionally since 1871, and hundreds of baseball cards are made for each player in the big leagues every single year. You can only imagine how much profit potential there is to be made from buying and selling baseball cards. And that's just baseball! The baseball card, sports trading card, and non-sports trading card market is a treasure trove ready to be discovered and exploited by Garage Sale Millionaires everywhere.

The sports trading card market includes every sports trading card manufactured. Non-sports trading cards consist of television and movie trading cards, entertainment trading cards, pro- wrestling trading cards, and various stiffeners from cigarette packs, dating from the late 1800s through the early 1900s. Although football, basketball, and hockey are all viable sports trading card markets, and non-sports cards are still a novelty in comparison to sports trading cards, the baseball card market continues to be the most lucrative.

Some of the top grading companies in this field are **Professional Sports Authenticator (PSA)** (www.psacard.com), **Beckett Grading Service (BGS)** (www.beckett.com), **GMA Grading** (www.gmagrading.com), and **Sports Card Guarantee (SGC)** (www.gosgc.com). By choosing to get your cards professionally graded, you'll increase the value of your card; it will be expertly authenticated and protected in a sturdy and durable card holder. Baseball cards are unique in the world of collectibles. Only baseball cards are graded based on three, very specific criteria:

> **The physical condition of the cards**—Is the card in good condition or mint condition?

> **The star quality of the player**—A rookie card of Babe Ruth is much more valuable than a rookie card of John Kruk.

> **When a player played the game**—Older cards of superstar players will be more valuable, overall, than cards for superstars who have played the game of baseball within the last few years.

Besides grading a baseball card on the star quality of a player and what era that player played the game, baseball grading companies use four criteria to grade the physical quality of a card. According to **BaseballCardBuyer.com**, the basic criteria for grading baseball cards are *Centering, Corners, Edges*, and *Surface*.

Centering—This refers to the evenness of the white space or border (if any) around the baseball card's main image. Centering is measured left to right and top to bottom and is defined in percentages. For example, if a card is slightly off-center (to the right) and way off-center (to the bottom), grading might be 55-45 and 65-35. That means that, to the naked eye, the baseball card's left border is just noticeably wider than the right border, but the top border is almost twice as wide as the bottom border.

Corners—This refers to both the sharpness of the corners and any creases in the corners. Dinged corners will drop the value of a baseball card more quickly than almost any other factor. It's a good thing if the corners are very sharp to the naked eye. Experts at professional card-grading companies check corners under magnification for complete accuracy. Some unscrupulous sellers will re-cut a card, which gives it sharp, new corners. This trick is easily detected with a metal template cut to the exact size at which that particular card was originally manufactured.

Edges—While not as important a factor in grading baseball cards as the previous two items, chipped edges will reduce a card's value. The two causes of imperfect edges are poor card cutting at the time the card was originally manufactured, and edge damage, due to extensive or improper handling. Of course, there's nothing you can do about how well the card was made, but you can reduce handling damage by keeping valuable baseball cards in protective sleeves.

Surface—Surface refers to the coating on the image of the baseball card as well as, but to a lesser degree, the printing on the back of the card. Other than unacceptable problems—such as pinholes, tape, staples, or writing—the biggest de-valuation factor will be creases in the card, typically visible to the naked eye. The very rarest of baseball cards are not subject to the same stringent surface criteria, due to their age and uniqueness. Less obvious, but nearly as important, are scratches on the surface of the card. Scratches can be observed by the naked eye when held closely under a normal light bulb. You should also rotate the card so that the light hits it at different angles. Finally, you should also look for printed dots that are a different color than the area around them, which could also reduce the value of your card.

A perfect example of an item that was thought to be worth more than it was. Before we got it graded, we saw that they were going on eBay for almost $30,000 for a Gem Mint 10 card. We were expecting a Mint 7 or 8 worth around $5000. I excitedly sent the card to PSA for grading only to find out my card was a mere Very Good Mint 3. The last Mint 3 card to sell on eBay at the time of writing this was only valued at $344. I paid $120 to get it graded so now instead of a profit in the thousands I only made around two hundred on the sale. Sometimes you have to take the chance even if the results don't turn out how you expected.

Antique Firearms

If you're not familiar with how valuable the collectible and antique firearms market is, take one look at the auction listings on **GunBroker.com**. The amounts are staggering, and a real eye-opener. Many firearms sales start in the hundreds of dollars, and the prices increase until they hit six figures. Antique firearms are a hot commodity because of their steady popularity over the decades, and sales don't appear to be letting up anytime soon. Antique firearms values are based on the physical qualities of the firearm, as well as its provenance.

Provenance relates to the place of origin or earliest known history of an item. If a firearm can be tied to a historic person or event, the value of that item will increase immensely. However, proving an item's history is not easy to do. Undisputable proof must be provided—not just word of mouth that the item has been passed down from a family member who claims they received the item from an important historical figure—instead, you will need substantial documentation to support the claims that the fire-arm is tied to a historically important event or person. If you have acceptable proof, chances are that you will be able to get a great price from action houses or even the right collector. The greater the significance of the historic event or person, the greater the potential value of the item. The **National Firearms Museum** (www.nramuseum.org/gun-info-research/pieces-of-history), sponsored by the National Rifle Association (NRA), is an excellent source of information regarding antique and historical firearms.

Many businesses are available to appraise firearms. Besides provenance information, appraisers may use a certain set of criteria to determine if a firearm has value:

Desirability/Aesthetics—People collect weapons that personally appeal to them and weapons that have a desirable aesthetic quality. This is not to say that an ugly, yet unique firearm will not be sought after. It's more of a general statement regarding what most collectors look for.

Condition—Condition definitely makes or breaks the value of any collectible. Now, thanks to the National Firearms Museum, a gun collector has a very sophisticated grading system at their disposal. Since grading remains a subjective art, there will always be differences in opinion as to the actual grade of an individual weapon. (Please see the charts later in this section for the NRA Standards for both modern and antique guns.)

Price—Most firearms have been cataloged and priced in various guides. A search on the internet can give you a good idea of the going rate for any particular weapon.

Maker/Manufacturer—Many collectors specialize according to manufacturer. The appeal and recognition of large name makers is typically much broader than the smaller, usually defunct, companies. Firearms bearing the trademarks of a reputable firm will usually have a larger collector base than a lesser-known maker.

Rarity—Not every old gun is rare and not every rare gun is old. If your gun is indeed rare, it will be of interest to someone, somewhere. The trouble is that often locating that special someone is just as difficult as finding the gun itself! Don't mistake rarity for desirability. Rarity is but one factor to consider when determining the value of a gun. Some collectors will only collect weapons that are in MIB (Mint in Box) condition and are not so interested in the rarity. Other collectors would do anything to have a rare gun in their collection, no matter what the condition...believe it or not! The original condition of an old gun is usually what is rare, not necessarily the gun itself.

Special Order Features—Firearms fall into a special category when it comes to special features. Almost every gun manufacturer has numerous options available to the buyer. From engraving, wood carving, checkering, special finishes, sights, and everything in between, there are literally hundreds of special features in the firearm world. To top it all off, not all of these special features were completed at the factory. Many were custom, after-market options. All these features must be taken into consideration when determining the collectible value of your weapon. What is desirable to one collector may not necessarily intrigue another.

Market/Economic Factors—In North America, we usually talk about firearm values in relation to the U.S. marketplace; however, even within the United States, the value of a particular gun can be quite different from region to region. This is particularly true at gun shows. Dealers notice higher demands for certain types of weapons in different states.

The ability to post your gun for sale online has rapidly removed the barriers typical of gun shows. For the person who has the funds available, this is the best time to buy. It's supply and demand in its purest form.

The NRA Modern Gun Condition Standards:

Grade	Condition
Fair	In safe working condition, but well worn, perhaps requiring replacement of minor parts or adjustments that should be indicated in advertisement; no rust, but may have corrosion pits that do render the gun unsafe or inoperable.
Good	In safe working condition; minor wear on working surfaces; no broken parts; no corrosion or pitting that will interfere with proper functioning.
Very Good	In perfect working condition; no appreciable wear on working surfaces; no corrosion or pitting; only minor surface dents or scratches.
Excellent	New condition; used very little; no noticeable marring of wood or metal; bluing perfect (except at muzzle or sharp edges).
Perfect	In new condition in every respect.
New	Not previously sold at retail; in same condition as current factory production.

NRA Antique Firearm Condition Standards:

Grade	Condition
Poor	Major and minor parts replaced; major replacement parts required and extensive restoration needed; metal deeply pitted; principal lettering, numerals and design obliterated; wood badly scratched, bruised, cracked or broken; mechanically inoperative; generally undesirable as a collectors' firearm.
Fair	Some major parts replaced; minor replacement parts may be required; metal rusted, may be lightly pitted all over, vigorously cleaned or re-blued; rounded edges of metal and wood; principal lettering, numerals and design on metal partly obliterated; wood scratched, bruised, cracked or repaired where broken; in fair working order or can be easily repaired and placed in working order.
Good	Some minor replacement parts; metal smoothly rusted or lightly pitted in places, cleaned or re-blued; principal letters, numerals and design on metal legible; wood refinished, scratched, bruised, or minor cracks repaired; in good working order.
Very Good	All original parts; none to 30% original finish; original metal surfaces smooth with all edges sharp; clear lettering, numerals and design on metal; wood slightly scratched or bruised; bore disregarded for collectors' firearms.
Fine	All original parts; over 30% original finish; sharp lettering, numerals and design on metal and wood; minor marks in wood; good bore.
Excellent	All original parts; over 80% original finish; sharp lettering, numerals and design on metal and wood; unmarred wood; fine bore.

Now You Know the Rest of the Story

The best decision you can make to guarantee that you receive proper value for your collectible items at resale is to have your items graded. There are two directions you can take to have your collectible items graded: self-grading or hiring a professional. When you are ready to sell your valuable treasures, be it in person or online, all your potential customers will want to know everything there is to know about what you are trying to sell. All this is accomplished through the process of grading. By providing your customers with as much detail as possible about your items, you will have a much better chance to complete every sale and make the most money.

CHAPTER 8

Downsizing, and How to Make Money Doing It

Downsizing is the current catchphrase for the older, sixty-plus crowd—or, truly, anyone who wants to be more mobile in life. I see it as an opportunity for someone to make some money. A lot of people don't think their stuff has any value. Maybe they think they can donate it and get a small write-off, but even that isn't worth it. I'm here to tell you that everything in your house has value. Let's talk about how we can benefit from it.

If you have kids, one of the hottest ways to make money is to sell the clothes, toys, and car seats that they've grown out of. You name it—if the age range is from baby to young adult, it has good value. Let's talk about Legos, for example. If you're anything like me, you have hundreds of pounds of Legos in your house.

My son is addicted to them. They have cost me a small fortune over the years—until I found out I could buy them used. Used Legos sell for $15 to $18 a pound and, if you're smart, you'll sell the mini figures separately. Some of them can be worth anywhere from $5 to $100, so do your research before you lump them together with the blocks.

If you have a lot of clothes, consider your target market to determine how best to sell them. Many different stores just resell baby and kids' clothing, and they are easily located by googling "consignment kids' clothes." Some of these stores will pay you outright for your items, while others will pay you on consignment as they sell.

If you are anything like my wonderful wife, you probably have beautiful clothes that you can't wear anymore, for whatever reason, but you don't have the heart to throw them away. At our house, we put high-end labels in high-end secondary stores—which, right now, are everywhere. If you type into Google, "upscale consignment clothes," you will get many shops that take name-brand, slightly used clothes, shoes, and bags, and resell them for you. With that being said, high-end shoes and purses will make you more money if you sell them on eBay. While these items *will* sell in a garage sale, you will get pennies on the dollar for them, so I wouldn't recommend it unless you're under a time constraint.

> ### Million $Tip
>
> When selling items, on Craigslist, Nextdoor, Facebook Marketplace, or any other local apps, make sure to always have somebody with you when people want to look at or buy your item.

Once you buy any type of furniture, aside from antiques, the value plummets. Consequently, when you are looking to buy furniture, it is always better to look for pieces that are slightly used. Use apps like Nextdoor, Facebook Marketplace, and Craigslist to search for used furniture being sold in your area. Once you find something you like, heavily negotiate for that item.

I guarantee that the market is flooded with furniture. Usually, when people sell it, they are in a rush to get it out of the house and will take pennies on the dollar in return. With that being said, if you have furniture to sell, I recommend the online marketplace as the best platform for those items.

If you have pool tables, jukeboxes, ping pong tables, pinball machines—or anything like that—I would recommend using game exchange stores. You take your item, drop it off, and they sell it for you. You can try the apps I recommended earlier as well, but I would call your local consignment game store first, to see if they will buy it outright or help you determine what you could get for that item. If you have a high-end pinball machine, eBay could be a great place for it—pinball machines do garner a lot of money.

A lot of people buy hot tubs and don't know what to do with them when they're moving, so they consider just leaving them. Hot tubs have real value, and I

> **Million $ Tip**
>
> Remember, to reference how many items have sold for on eBay, open an advanced search and apply the following filter: find "Show Only" in the left-hand menu, then select "Completed Items." Your search results will give you a national valuation of that item, and a good comparison on what other people will pay for it.

recommend that you try to sell them first, before just leaving them behind. Guaranteed, you will make anywhere from $500 to $4,000, depending on the brand and condition of your hot tub. In this economy, every little bit helps! The same goes for outdoor playsets. The apps that I mentioned earlier are great places to offer up

large, difficult-to-move items. You want to make sure, with anything you're selling—playset, hot tub, furniture—that when you list your items, you provide great pictures. A lot of them. Always list the name brand of the item, if there is one, and be sure to list the size of the item too. Detailed photographs and accurate information will guarantee you a better chance of selling your item than if you left these important pieces of information out of your listing.

We *all* have great sporting equipment that we had the best intentions of using but never got a chance. Or maybe you did use it, but it's still in great condition. Many different stores sell used sporting equipment and, believe it or not, depending on the brand, sport, and time of year that you sell or consign your items, you could make a pretty penny. Sporting equipment can also be sold through the local online marketplaces, and even on eBay, so make sure, before you consign it or put a low valuation on it, that you go to eBay and find out what your item has sold for in the past.

A lot of people have antiques and, when people are downsizing, they are often among the first items that need to be sold.

Many people believe that their antiques are worth a lot of money. Unfortunately, currently, and for the foreseeable future, there is a glut on the market. A lot of antique stores are not even taking these items unless they're very rare, or highly collectible—which is only about 5%-10% of all antiques.

If you do not know the value of your antique, call your local antique store and see if they can come out to your house to give you an appraisal. Let them know that you are interested in selling these items. However, if you want an appraisal just to hold onto for your insurance company, you must let them know that ahead of time. Your appraisal, and what the antique store will give you on the spot, will be two hugely different dollar amounts.

So, you have a lot of books—great! I have a way of making money

Million $ Tip

Not all books need to be extremely old to have a big value. For example, the first edition of Alcoholics Anonymous, published in 1939 by Works Publishing Company, is worth thousands of dollars. An unsigned copy can go anywhere from $4,500 to $37,500+ depending on the condition.

from them. In Chapter 1, I told you about apps that allow you to scan the barcode on the back of a book with your cell phone to see the valuation. There are several sites, like Amazon, where you can sell used books. Countless bookstores will take them on consignment or buy them outright. If the book is an older first edition, and/or signed, you will want to check the valuation on eBay. Good books have huge value, and they can make you a lot of money—but you need to do your research.

Old computers and televisions have very little value. As a matter of fact, a lot of charities will not accept these items, nor will landfills (i.e. putting them in your trash can). There *are* places that recycle these items in big cities but be prepared; you may have to spend some time searching for nearby communities that can do so. Be sure to check your local government websites for any upcoming safe disposal events, where members of the community can bring electronics, batteries, and chemicals—anything that cannot go into the trash—for recycling or safe disposal. TVs and laptops that are 2-3 years old still have some value and can be sold through the local channels discussed earlier.

Appliances, depending on their age and overall condition, can definitely be sold through many online marketplaces. However, if they're more than three or four years old and not in good condition, your only option may be to hire someone to cart them away. If you do not want to pay to have them removed, a long-shot recommendation would be to put them out by your trash. There are always people in big cities that come around and snatch up stuff like that for scrap metal. This way, you can still unload your unwanted appliances, and it will not cost you any money to have them removed.

What About Everything Else?

Believe it or not, downsizing can be as simple as returning a neighbor's rake or ladder or turning in library books and other items that you have on loan, from either a store or a friend. So do go through those items—if you stumble upon something that you're renting, good chance you're now past the due date and you don't want to incur any new fees. If you do have fees, simple kindness can work wonders on getting those waived.

If you find an item that you don't need or want, and it's still in its original packaging, I would try to take it back. I have a better than 50-50 success rate with stores taking back an unopened item and giving me what I paid for it. Remember, the item needs to be in its *original* packaging and in perfect condition in order for this to work, and the seller usually needs to be a national brand or big box store—like Costco, Home Depot, Lowe's, or Target. You have absolutely nothing to lose and everything to gain. And don't think that you're out of luck if you're past the 30- or 60-day return window. Some stores will give you cash back; others will give you credit. Either way, you're getting full value for that item.

There are going to be items that you come across that one family member will want to get rid of, and another family member will not. It happens to me every time I put on a garage sale with my wife and son. The way I get around this particular conflict is very simple. After the family picks all of the items to sell at the garage sale, or to get rid of before we move, everybody is

> **Million $ Tip**
>
> If you have a lot of friends on Facebook, let them know that you're downsizing and getting ready to sell your items. You can probably make a little bit more money from people that you know over random strangers.

allowed to take one or two pieces back to keep, no questions asked. It's a great way of handling the difficult emotions that can come up, especially when someone realizes they want to keep an item that they've only just rediscovered in the process of cleaning out the house. My last piece of advice on this: if a loved one really wants it, don't force them to get rid of it. This will cause long-term

You're also going to unearth many items that have little to no value, for example: magazines and older newspapers. Unless the newspaper is pre-1900s, it will almost certainly have little or no value. You *can* check the value on eBay for certain magazine issues or titles but, without even knowing what you have, I am confident that most of the magazines and newspapers you've been collecting are worthless. My recommendation is to recycle them so that they don't end up in a landfill. Used mattresses need to be thrown away; due to the bed bug epidemic, nobody wants them. Drop-down cribs are dangerous and most of them are on recall, so please do not sell these items. Take them apart and throw them away.

Now that you've gone through all your items and tried to sell everything you want to sell, you may still have items sitting in your garage and you just don't know what to do with them. There are several great charities, with a legitimate 501-C3 number given to them by the IRS, that manage thrift stores—like Goodwill, AMVETS (American Veterans Thrift Stores), ARC, and Salvation Army.

A 501-C3 is the designation that the Internal Revenue Service gives to all non-profit charities. If you donate money or goods to these charities, you can write it off on your taxes. For everybody, the amount will be a little bit different, so please check with your accountant; make sure you get a receipt every time you donate. Understand that this is so much better than throwing away your unwanted items. What could be trash for you could be a new start for someone else. Make sure you not only list all the items that you are donating, but you also need to take a photo of them. Also keep any receipts you have on the items you are donating, just in case you are audited.

CHAPTER 9

Putting on the World's Greatest Garage Sale

My lifelong fascination with garage sales began at a very young age. I was only nine years old when I held my first sale with my mom. I didn't really know why I even wanted to hold a garage sale. I saw other families in my neighborhood having garage sales, but I just didn't quite get it. What was the big deal, anyway? At nine years old, it seemed as though people were going through a lot of trouble and effort for nothing. Since garage sales were usually held on a Saturday and Sunday—usually *all-day* Saturday and Sunday—that meant the sale took away a chunk of some very serious playtime. Why would I ever want to sacrifice having lots of fun? What a boring way to waste the weekend!

It couldn't have been about the money. The concept of free market economics—buying and selling physical goods for money and hopefully turning a profit—was just barely starting to sink in at such a young age.

However, I did notice one common characteristic shared by all the families who did hold garage sales. Every single one of our neighbors seemed to be having serious amounts of fun! Of course, being nine years old, I wanted to have fun too! After a lengthy discussion with my mom, I convinced her we needed to have some fun like the neighbors, so we should have a garage sale of our own. My mom agreed, and my first garage sale was a go.

This beautiful military appointment, signed by President Abraham Lincoln, was bought through an online auction for $6,200. I had it personally framed, and now it sits in my office as one of my favorite presidential signatures that I own.

Million $ Tip

If you want to have a garage sale and have just one day for such an event, make sure you hold your sale on a Saturday. As a second option, try to choose a Friday.

Between Friday and Saturday, you'll get the most traffic possible. People tend to not attend garage sales between Sunday and Thursday like they do on Fridays and Saturdays. On these other weekdays, you will just be spinning your wheels and wasting your time, hard work, and effort.

After my first sale ever was over, I finally understood why everyone seemed to be having so much fun. I also learned my first worldly lesson. In the end, it really was all about the money! People actually came and gave us handfuls of cash for a bunch of old stuff that we didn't want anyway. I can't remember how much my mother and I made at our first sale together, but I do remember seeing more cash than I had ever seen before in my life. Safe to say, I was immediately hooked on the idea of holding garage sales. I had been bitten by the garage sale bug and bitten badly. A new world seemed to open for me. After all these years, I still can't wait for the arrival of summer so I can have yet another sale!

The Need-To-Know List:

Essential Information for Holding the World's Greatest Garage Sale

There are certain things you need to know to hold a successful, money-making garage sale. In this section, I will discuss some of the key elements necessary for making your garage sale the best it can be.

When to Hold the Sale

One of the most crucial elements in conducting a successful garage sale is knowing the right time to host one. Picking the right days of the week to conduct your sale is absolutely critical.

You really need to hold your garage sale when as many people as possible can attend. The more foot traffic you can generate at your sale, the better chance you have of success and, of course, turning substantial profits. Well, timing, and having some seriously cool things to sell, but I will discuss that later in the chapter. The best day to hold a garage sale is Saturday. Sunday through Thursday are generally not good days at all to have a sale. You will waste plenty of time and effort on any of these days. While some people may show up if your sale is on or after Sunday, most people have other obligations that will take priority. On Sunday, the priority will be attending church and family events. During the week, the obvious priority will be work. This doesn't mean you won't have some success on other days of the week, but usually, the highest number of sales will be made on Saturdays.

If you insist on having a sale on a weekday, pick Friday. Friday is an excellent secondary day to hold a garage sale. Some people might take Friday off as part of a three-day weekend, and some good sales may be made—providing you publicize your sale with street signs, and on community websites such as Facebook, Nextdoor, or Craigslist. Even if your neighbors don't take the whole day off, by Friday afternoon they may leave work early and be ready to get a jump on finding great sales in their area. If you want to host a two-day garage sale, definitely plan for a Friday and Saturday.

If you live in a place with four distinct seasons, it's best to schedule your sales during the warm weather months. That means anytime during the late spring, throughout summer, or into the early

> **Million $ Tip**
>
> Never have a garage sale on Labor Day, Memorial Day, or any major holiday. Your sales will be cut in half!

fall. Scheduling your garage sale for a potentially non-rainy day is also key to success.

You can usually rely on the accuracy of advanced local weather predictions up to a week in advance. Many people just don't attend garage sales when the weather is bad. If you live in a part of the country that has great weather all year long, then every weekend offers you the potential for garage sale success and profitability.

Getting People to Your Garage Sale—and Managing Them Once They've Arrived

Getting as many people as possible to attend your garage sale is a key component for achieving financial success. Additionally, how you advertise and inform your customers is a critical factor in making your garage sale more profitable.

> **Million $ Tip**
>
> Half the fun of going to any garage sale is doing the buying. But people also want to be entertained! No, you do not have to do cartwheels, juggle, or put on a magic show. All you must do is be kind, chatty, and make the process for the buyer an enjoyable experience. I guarantee if you are a great garage sale host, people will buy more of your wares and will come back when they know you are having another sale.

Many individuals plan their entire weekend solely around going to garage sales. When they see a sign or advertisement for your garage sale, they may arrive at a minimum, ninety minutes early. If you think I'm kidding, just wait until you have your first sale. For as long as I've been involved in the business, and too many times to count, I've seen people actually camp out in the seller's front yard before the sun even rises so that they can be the first ones there. Even if your sign states that the sale doesn't start until 9:00 AM, people will still get there while you're setting it up. Even when you're pulling items out of your garage to place on the sale tables, they will be walking with you, trying to carry on a conversation, and may even ask if they can help you set it up. Experienced garage sale shoppers do this to not only get a look at what you have to sell but also place themselves in the best position to have the first pick at all of your great sale items.

How you handle garage sale early birds is important, because these early arrivals could make or break your garage sale. Don't shoo them away like my mother always wanted to—and did, on many occasions. I suppose she just didn't understand the business as well as I did, even at a young age. As a child, I wanted to let all my early bird customers into our house and have them start picking up our furniture and taking it home with them. For a price, of course! Enjoy your customers, even if they prove to be difficult to handle. People like to shop in a jovial environment. Definitely make sure you hold a garage sale that has an element of fun attached to it. In many cases, a garage sale with a relaxed shopping and sales environment equals bigger profits! I will discuss some of the ways to spice up a garage sale later in this chapter.

Preparation and Setup

How do you prepare for and set everything up for the world's greatest garage sale? You need to arrange the details for your sale a few weeks, not just days, in advance. If you want to make the highest profit possible, you need to make sure everything is in order and ready to go before the sale begins. This, of course, takes a little bit of planning.

Having a garage sale is a great opportunity for you to go room to room—closet to closet, drawer to drawer—throughout your home, to identify all the items for which you have no need or use any longer. This includes unwanted gifts and things you may never have liked or needed at all. Have you used, worn, or even looked at something you have tucked away collecting dust in the past year? If not, then you more than likely need to get rid of it. If something doesn't sell, donate it. Never throw away anything before the sale! You can sell almost anything, believe me—I have seen it all.

I truly believe that if you can find all the stuff in your house you don't use, you can make very good money from it. If, for some reason, you sell something and decide you need it again, go to the store and buy it new again. Or go to another garage sale and buy it!

Million $ Tip

You will want to try to inform the customers at your garage sale about the history behind the items you are trying to sell. The amount of information you do or do not provide could make or break a sale! Customers at garage sales absolutely love hearing background stories, and value adding information, about the items they are getting ready to buy.

I usually begin preparing for my garage sales about a month before the actual date of the sale so that I can be thorough in my preparations (this is not necessary—just being thorough. You can pull it together in a week!). I want to make sure I've gone through my house from top to bottom, so I don't overlook something of value I can sell.

The worst thing that can happen is that you discover things you could have sold after your garage sale is history. After I've exhausted the search throughout my home for saleable items, I move on to my office and look for even more items to sell.

Parents, family members, neighbors, and friends are fantastic sources for finding valuable items to sell at any garage sale. Over time, miscellaneous items always seem to get stuck in people's basements and, as a result, all those long-forgotten items just end up gathering dust and cobwebs. Always ask people you know if there's anything of theirs you can put in your garage sale. You can always arrange to split the money you make on their items with them. It really is a win-win situation for all involved. They give you their old stuff; you do all the work. They make a percentage of the sales! Many times, family and friends want to help you out, and will even work at your garage sale because these events are so much fun.

Through the years, I've developed a proven timeline to help me get ready for any garage sale and stay organized. By always adhering to my timeline, I can 99.99% guarantee myself that everything I want to sell

---

Million $ Tip

Use websites like Nextdoor and Craigslist to advertise your garage sale. You can also use them to find all of the great garage sales in your area. They are an excellent resource for all garage sale fanatics.

will be at my garage sale.

Let's look at the timeline and then I will discuss some key points in more detail.

Key Elements from My Tried-and-True Garage Sale Timeline

I cannot tell you how many garage sales I've seen where people will slow down, stick their heads out the car window, take a look around, and keep driving. This is definitely not what you want to have happen at your sales.

One Month Before the Sale: Size Matters

To make sure your garage sale is an even bigger eye-catcher, you'll want to have as many items on display as you can and have them spread out on as many tables as possible. By having enough tables to display all your merchandise, your garage sale will look nice and big. Reload pictures of the front of the garage sale to social media accounts whenever something sells.

Million $ Tip

The more treasure, trinkets, and goodies you have in your garage sale, the bigger it will look. By having a fully stocked sale, your chances for garage sale success will increase exponentially. When people drive by and see a lot of great items at a garage sale, they will almost always stop, get out of their cars, and walk quickly into your sale.

When you have people driving by to see if your sale is worth the time and energy to even get out of their cars, bigger is most definitely better. Also, when you have a larger sale, people will take more time to browse and, eventually, to shop. In my decades of garage sale experience, the more time people spend at a garage sale, the more money they seem to spend.

By including as much stuff as you can from as many families as possible, the better opportunity you'll have to make a bigger profit.

One Month to Two Weeks Before the Sale: Clean and Fix Everything

Before your sale, make sure everything you plan to sell is clean and in working order. If you're selling stuffed animals, furniture with cushions, or even pillows, spray them with Febreze®! If something needs to be fixed, you need to fix it before the sale so you can avoid customers bargaining you way down on the price. There's nothing worse than going to a garage sale and finding something you really want to buy that is in absolutely awful shape. At this point, I have seen it all. Dirty, malfunctioning, and broken items don't bring in very much revenue!

The following is a list of things that are deal breakers for me:

- If items look dusty, unclean, and noticeably in a state of ill repair, I will pass on buying, even if there is an inkling that I could later sell them for a profit.

- Items that physically fall apart in my hands when I pick them up get a pass from me every time.

- Once, when I went to plug an electrical item into an outlet, the item for sale started smoking...no thanks.

- I've found items that smelled so horrible they were a complete turn- off...a definite NO!

- I've found rusted-out items that lost all their value many years—or even decades—ago. It doesn't take a very keen eye to pick up on this.

Million $ Tip

There are several Household items like vinegar and Coca-Cola that can be used to remove rust from metal items! Just soak your rusted item in one of the solutions for a few hours or overnight, and then use a brush to scrub away the loosened rust.

My list could have been longer, but you get the idea. Always make sure the items you have are in decent working order. People will ask you to plug in an item to see if it really works, and they will pick up items to see if they fall apart. The opportunity to get the most money for every item lies in whether or not it's in proper working order, and how good it looks when it's sitting on the sales table. If you have something to sell and it's missing a part, believe me, your garage sale visitors are going to ask if you have that missing part. It is an inevitable garage sale truth...they will always ask! If you happen to have the part, it will usually guarantee the sale. If not, then good luck.

Customers will ask you questions you never thought they would come up with in a million years. Be ready for anything and always be honest with your reply. If you are dishonest at any time during your sale, the buyer will be upset. If you ever have another garage sale, they will not stop by again. More importantly, they could warn others to stay away from any garage sale you hold in the future.

One Month Before Sale: Locate Original Packaging

It's very important, especially if you're selling collectibles, to include the original box or packaging that came with the item. Why? Items with the original packaging, along with the instructions (if there were any), will sell for much more money than items being sold without. A lot more money! In my experience, an item with its original packaging will sell for at least 20% to 40% more than an item sold by itself. If you're selling a collectible, the original box and certificate will raise the value by about 50%. If your collectible came with a wind-up key, it is essential to find that key to keep the item fully intact and functional. It is crucial to include anything you can find that could help add value to your sale item.

It's worth your while and will result in bigger profits, to take the extra time needed to make certain everything is in perfect order for your big day. Do everything in your power to present the world's greatest garage sale. Run your event like a well-oiled machine and your pocketbook, as well as your bank account, will be happy that you did.

One Week Before the Sale: Price Your Items

Pricing is another critical element of any garage sale. *To place prices on items or put them out without pricing…that is the question.* You would think prices should be placed on everything at a garage sale. This is not always the case.

I've gone to a multitude of garage sales where items for sale fall into two categories... items with pricing and items without any price attached.

Million $ Tip

When someone is trying to buy one of your treasures, they are going to ask questions. Sometimes many questions! Try to give as many answers as you can and do not ever rush them. This kind of interaction is considered great entertainment for garage sale enthusiasts and is truly what garage sale customers look forward to every weekend. If you are short with them, treat them unkindly, and show disinterest, I can guarantee they will not buy anything, and they will never come back to another one of your garage sales.

Why would someone not put a price on something at a garage sale? By not placing a price on an item, the seller forces a potential buyer to personally inquire about the price, or to make an offer, giving the seller some leeway in determining the price. Non-pricing of items occurs most often with items of very little value. With less expensive items selling for as little as a dollar or less, it will take you hours to price out everything. On these types of items, try omitting the price altogether and bargaining with your customers.

You're not going to make much from these items anyway. You know people are going to probably spend the minimum, so why waste your valuable time marking a price

Million $ Tip

Have an extension cord available for customers to use if you are selling any electrical items. Your customers may want to test them out before they buy.

on small insignificant items?

When pricing items, don't be greedy. If you're too greedy with your pricing, people will walk away from your sale with nothing in hand.

Place a fair price on your items but always leave yourself some room to bargain. If you have an item that cost $100 when it was new, your sale price should not exceed $45, and you should be ready to accept $30. If you're not prepared to take an offer of $30 for the item, then slightly raise your sale price to $47, $48, or even $50. Remember, the goal at any garage sale is to have nothing left over at the end of the day. Try to sell everything on hand so you can begin building fresh new inventory for your next sale.

If you're unsure of something when it comes to pricing your sale items, search on eBay. eBay will give you an up-to-the-minute idea of what an item is worth. If an item is worth only a few dollars, price it to sell. It's better to put it on your table and have someone make an offer than to hold onto it for another ten years!

If you really don't know how to value an item, offer it at what you believe to be a fair price and be very observant of your customers during your sale. If someone wants to buy an item you marked at a certain

> **Million $ Tip**
>
> Always leave room for "bargaining" when pricing an item. Make sure you price your sale items 15% to 20% higher than the minimum price you would accept; then you can negotiate the price when someone makes an offer.

price and it looks like they are ready to walk away from the sale, go over and ask, "Would you like to make me an offer?" If they come up with a number that's below the price you had listed for the item, counteroffer. You can always suggest meeting in the middle—between your final price and your customer's offer. If they offer $2 and you make a final counteroffer of $3, then $2.50 will be the final sales price. That's the normal flow of the garage sale.

There are so many opportunities for people to buy new merchandise at great prices. New means items are in perfect or nearly perfect condition. New may also mean this year's model. I can guarantee you that almost every item sold at a garage sale is not going to be this year's latest model. Even if an item is in perfect condition, you can't expect to make all your money back or consider charging retail value. Don't forget! You are conducting a garage sale, where your customers will seldom pay full price. That's just the way it works. You're doing extremely well if you get between 25% and 35%, or sometimes even 45%, of what you originally paid for an item.

When you're thinking about what's valuable and what could be worth good money at your garage sale, don't consider used books. If you charge more than $2 to $4 per book, people will quickly walk away. No sale, my friends! Used books don't hold much value unless they're old, 1st edition, or signed. Computers, old appliances, and tube televisions don't sell for much, either. Of course, you can always try to sell these items. Just be cognizant of what you might—or, more than likely, might not—get for older items way past their prime.

One of the reasons you should try to sell everything you can has to do with trash removal. Whatever you have left after your sale that needs to be disposed of will cost you money to haul away. Trash companies won't even take the majority of larger items that you were unable to sell, and you'll be forced to hire a private junk hauler to get rid of your items for you. Trash companies also don't like taking obsolete computer monitors and printers or anything that could be considered hazardous to a dump site. Secondhand stores no longer take everything readily, as they once did. In the end, you'll be stuck spending your hard-earned garage sale profits hiring a hauler to move anything that wasn't sold. It's sometimes better to take lower offers for your sale items so you don't have to dispose of them yourself at the end of the day.

Always remember that *a garage sale may not be the answer.* High- end clothes, shoes, and purses will do better at a high-end consignment store. See what they offer before the sale; not everything will be accepted at these stores. Kids' clothes, toys, and furniture should also be taken to consignment stores. In big cities, some stores specialize in kids' stuff. High-end collectibles and jewelry will do better on eBay.

Two Weeks through Two Days Before the Sale: Advertising Your Garage Sale

Your sale items have all been exhaustively acquired, painstakingly organized for your garage sale, and are all ready to go. They are priced, cleaned up, and looking good...as though they are ready to literally leap from that table into your customers' hands. Now, all you have to do is figure out a way to get people to your sale.

> **Million $ Tip**
>
> Check your HOA to make sure you are allowed to have a garage sale. Some counties require you to get a permit first.

From my experience, most people believe that advertising a garage sale is an extremely complicated process. Nothing could be further from the truth. Advertising for your garage sale is the easiest aspect of the sales process. Publicizing your garage sale does take some attention to complete, but it's a very straightforward exercise.

Two weeks before your sale, you need to start taking advantage of the many free advertising resources at your disposal. Your advertising must all be in place a couple of days before your target day. Not only are most of these resources free of charge, but they are also very effective, proven methods for making your forthcoming event known. These free resources include:

- **Advertising on the Internet.** Many garage sale websites will let you post your garage sale information for free.

- **Various Social Networking Websites** such as **Facebook, X, Instagram, Nextdoor,** and **Craigslist.**

- **Flyers at Local Libraries, Coffee Shops, and Your Neighborhood Recreation Centers.** Always be sure to get permission to place your garage sale advertisements so that your hard work will not be torn down and thrown in the trash before your sale.

The week before your sale, you need to start posting details on Twitter. Three days before your sale, you must have it posted on Craigslist. Within a few days of your sale, you need to have everything ready to share on Facebook.

You will need to begin creating all the signs for your sale one week prior. These signs will be placed around your immediate area and the surrounding neighborhoods.

They need to be placed in designated, high-traffic locations within twelve hours of your garage sale.

The higher and faster the traffic in your area, the bigger your signs should be. I recommend obtaining white poster boards from an art or office supply store. You can even try going to a frame store—they often have tons of scrap mat board that you might be able to get for free. You also need to make your signs extremely visible. Choose boards that are either red or white. For lettering, use thick-tipped magic markers. If you're using a red board, always use a black magic marker. Green or brown colors get lost in the background of trees and yards.

If you're placing signs in speedy traffic areas, you'll want to use big mat boards. When I say big, I mean BIG! I am talking posters at least 3' high x 3' wide. If you're in an area where people use pedestrian walkways to leisurely walk with their children or dogs, or go out for their daily jog, then you can use smaller signs to advertise your sale.

Time Before Sale	Things To Do
Two Weeks	Start looking for and gathering up items you do not use from around your house and office.
	Ask your family members if they have any items for you to sell.
	Try to get as many items as possible for your sale.
	Size matters!
One Week	Create your signs. Extra credit points are awarded for very colorful and eye-catching signs and flyers.
	Get a change purse or fanny pack together so you are prepared to make the correct change once your garage sale starts. Make sure to have lots of quarters, and $1, $5 and $10 bills on hand.
	To get the word out on the date and location of your garage sale, start posting on social networking websites about five days before your sale. Make sure to post details on Craigslist, Instagram, Facebook, and Nextdoor.
	Relist your sale on social media two days prior to the event.
The Night Before	Start methodically pricing your sale items. Never sell something if you do not know the value!
	Make sure you have enough tables for all of your sale items.
	If necessary, have a power cord set up for your sale.
The Morning Of	Put your signs out in the busiest traffic areas in your community and around your neighborhood—locations where you believe the highest volume of people will see your announcement. Do this in the early morning before the sale, so competing garage sales don't tear them down.
	Two hours before your start time, begin physically setting up your garage sale.
Your Sale Beings	**Smile and watch the money pour in!**
After	Take all items that aren't sold to a 501 c3 charity donation center, such as Goodwill, VA Store, and so on.
	Pull down any signs or announcements you physically put up, and remove your posts from social media, or else people will continue to try to contact you about your sale

I recommend making about 20 signs and placing them on busy streets within one to three miles of your home. Be sure to take a staple gun with you, as well as some duct tape. Never put your signs on traffic markers — that is against the law. Take the signs to as many busy streets as close to your home as possible. By placing the majority of your signs near stop signs or stop lights, people will have ample time to read them. If libraries, grocery stores, or shopping malls are within three to five miles of your home, then these are also great places to put up signs. Be sure to place these signs near the parking lot exits as well.

Don't place signs in locations where traffic is moving very fast and streaking past. When you place a sign along a busy street, and the cars are going about 45+ mph, what are the chances anyone is going to even see that garage sale sign? The answer is little to none.

What should be written on your signs to achieve the best financial results at your sale? The address is the most important piece of information and needs to be listed first. The day and time of your sale go directly under the address. Then, with bullet points, include some key items you will have at the sale. Be focused. Only list the five most sought-after, best-selling items. Anything more and your sign gets too crowded.

People often make the big mistake of trying to squeeze too much information onto a sign. Here are the top items people sell, and what people look for most at garage sales — when these items are listed on a garage sale sign, people take notice, and will make it a point to stop and spend their money:

- Antiques
- Electronics
- Baby anything (i.e. clothes, bibs, toys)

251

- Bikes
- Tools
- Collectibles
- Furniture

Extras to Have at Your Sale that Will Help It Achieve World's Greatest Garage Sale Status

A Refreshment Stand

When people come to a garage sale, especially in the hot summer months, they're going to get thirsty. The larger your sale, the longer people will pause and spend time looking at as many items as they can. As a result, they will want something to drink. A refreshment stand at your sale will help make the experience for your guests a much better one. It may also put some extra money in your pocket because people will stay longer if they are not hungry or thirsty.

If you have children of your own or know some kids in the neighborhood, see if they want to have a lemonade or refreshment stand right next to your garage sale. Having kids selling soft drinks, iced tea, lemonade, and/or bottled water will save you from having to run into your house for a cup of water when someone inevitably asks for a drink. Also, consider selling food items at your refreshment stand. These items could include cookies, candy, chips, popcorn, or a variety of homemade baked goods. Shoppers will invariably be more relaxed and will have a more enjoyable time at your sale if they can quench their thirst and enjoy a snack!

Always remember that if your customers are enjoying themselves, there's a good chance that they will spend more time and more money on your sale. Just think, you don't need to pay for a babysitter and your kids will learn about money.

If you want to have a refreshment stand on a larger scale, contact your church or a local charity to see if they would like to host one at your garage sale. Good refreshment stands at garage sales easily net between $50 and $200. I've seen some refreshment stands take in almost as much as the garage sale itself.

More Tables Equal Better Profits

Earlier, I mentioned the necessity of having an adequate number of tables. When you hold your garage sale, you're going to need as many tables as possible to sufficiently display your items. The more tables you have, the better your garage sale becomes... it never fails. If you put all your items in boxes, potential customers will have to make an effort to rummage through everything. Sometimes people like that, but more often they don't. One of the most universal garage sale rules is that all items need to be laid out in plain sight. If you're asking for good money for your valued objects, you don't want to display them in a crowded pile or hidden in a box. If items are buried away, there's a very real chance someone might not even see what you're trying to sell. Having all your treasures nicely laid out is a monumental plus. This means you're going to need those tables I mentioned earlier to show off your wares.

My son, Logan, and his friends selling snacks and lemonade at a past garage sale.

When you put the tables out, people might ask if you're going to sell the tables as well as what's on each table. When I say everything must go at a garage sale, I am not joking! You will need to determine ahead of time if you want to sell the tables and at what price you will want to sell them. Of course, only sell them if they're yours and aren't borrowed. If you have really ugly looking tables, always cover them with attractive tablecloths. If you have items lying on top of an ugly, old, and weathered table without a proper covering, the items for sale will appear to be ugly too.

Volunteers

When your garage sale is quite large, one person working the sale just won't do. There's no chance you'll be able to cover everything and help every customer with just one person, especially if you have more than one family selling their treasures at your garage sale. This is where having multiple volunteers comes in handy. If there are several families selling items at your garage sale, then each family really needs to have two or more helpers present. There are a few positive reasons for this:

> ### Million $ Tip
>
> By inviting more people to help you at your garage sale, you increase your chances for garage sale success, and you will more than likely have a great turnout.

People usually come to garage sales in groups. There won't be anyone at your sale for a while and then, suddenly, you'll find yourself inundated with 5 to 15 people all at once. One person staffing your sale won't be able to provide the level of service your potential customers will require. As a result of being understaffed, you'll end up losing money.

Shoppers need ample time to look at everything. Not only that, but they are going to want to chitchat with you and negotiate the price on almost everything. If you rush them, they'll become dissatisfied with your sale and walk away without buying anything. At a large garage sale, it is good to have at least three volunteers standing by, ready to help, answer questions, and assist with getting items into shoppers' cars.

There is a really good chance if you sell something large it's going to take a little time to settle on a price and help load it into a customer's car or truck. Having a volunteer who can just hang out and talk with the other customers, process any sales, or just supervise the sale with help as needed (while you're busy helping others) will be a huge asset.

Location, Location. If you are in a small, hard-to-get-to neighborhood, think about moving the sale to a family member or friend's house. For example, if you have a family member who has a lot of stuff and lives next to a busy street, you may want to move the garage sale there.

What Not to Do at Your Garage Sale

Do Not Let Strangers into Your Home... EVER!

One piece of wisdom I want you all to know, and never forget, is **NEVER LET ANYONE INTO YOUR HOME UNDER ANY CIRCUMSTANCES.**

There are a few essential reasons why this is a good strategy:

People have been known to get into your house and case it. These strangers look over the contents of your home, see what they can find of value, and check how your home is laid out for easy access and a quick exit. This is commonly referred to as "casing the joint". Experienced thieves take everything they see into consideration so they can return later and rob you. Not good!

People have been known to come into your house and take items while you're distracted or when you're not paying attention. Again, not good!

The shoppers who come into your home to use the bathroom facilities might not be up to your level of cleanliness. The last thing you want to do is to clean up after a stranger who improperly uses your bathroom or makes a mess in your home. This goes way beyond not good!

As you can see from the previous examples, nothing good can result from letting strangers into your house. In advance of your garage sale, make up some plausible excuses you're comfortable using to avoid being in this situation. For example, you have a baby asleep inside, you have a sick parent, or you own a dog that doesn't really get along with strangers. Whatever the reason is, be prepared to convey it at a moment's notice.

Never Take Checks

It gets very difficult to turn down any sale, especially when you are talking hundreds of dollars. People will try to convince you the only form of payment they have at the moment is a personal check. Some customers will go to great lengths to reassure you their check is legitimate. If you accept a check from someone you don't know and it turns out to be no good, as is often the case, then you have only yourself to blame for your predicament. Not only will you have to pay your bank an NSF (Non-Sufficient Funds) fee for accepting a bad check, but you also get to keep the worthless check as a truly wonderful reminder of your sale. Avoid these problems by never accepting a personal check.

Million $ Tip

Cash is king, but you should be aware that counterfeit bills are all too common. I would recommend getting a counterfeit detection pen to test large bills before you accept them. You can buy a 3-pack, and peace of mind, for less than $10. If you make a mark on an authentic dollar bill, the ink will appear amber and eventually fade away; if the bill is suspect, the ink will turn black. You can also verify the authenticity of new $100 bills by checking for the presence of a security strip.

You just can't afford to accept checks from people frequenting garage sales. Unfortunately, it's very likely that they don't have the money in their account to cover the amount written. A possible sale-saving solution—for those experiencing financially rougher times—is to ask them for a small cash deposit instead of a check. Tell them you'll hold the item they want for 48 hours so they can get the money when their bank opens, or when they get paid.

If they don't return at a certain time, advise them that their deposit is non-refundable. To prevent them from disputing the deposit after the 48-hour window has passed, or if you feel they might demand their money back, write a very informal agreement and have them date and sign it. That way you're completely covered from a legal standpoint. Under no circumstances would I ever accept a check from someone I don't know.

Million $ Tip

Before your garage sale, make a sign to let your customers know that you take Venmo/PayPal. It's great if you have both. Be sure to include your Venmo/PayPal handle and then put the sign in a visible place throughout your event. This lets your customers know they can shop even if they don't have cash and can increase your sales by 15-20%! Plus, now you have an alternative option if someone tries to pay with a check.

The Cash Back Artist

One of the biggest rip-offs at garage sales is one I call the "Cash Back Artist". Many garage sales get very busy, and the owner of the garage sale can get somewhat overwhelmed and usually distracted. Customers are constantly asking you for details about this or that item or negotiating prices on what they want to buy—confusion reigns supreme.

Occasionally, you may have a customer who will ask you to take a check but then ask to write the check for more than the sale price of the item. The customer will then request the amount above the cost of the item be handed back to them in cash.

For example, a seemingly decent-looking, well-groomed shopper at your sale wants to buy a couch. You've priced the couch at $200. Then, the shopper says, very convincingly, "Oh, man, I don't have enough cash on me. I'm so sorry. When I left the house this morning, I thought I put enough cash in my wallet. I must have gotten busy, and I only have about $60 or $80 on me." The customer lets you see the actual cash in their wallet to suggest, subliminally, that you're dealing with what appears to be an honest person. "Can I write this check for $250 and could you give me the difference in cash?" The unknowing garage sale owner takes the check for the couch and feels good about the sale, but seven days later the check bounces. Congratulations.

Thanks to the Cash Back Artist you don't have your sofa, you are out an extra $50 in cash (that you handed out to the customer when you accepted his/her check), and you now owe your bank money to cover the NSF fees you accrued when the check bounced.

The Cash Back Artist may also use fake certified checks. This kind of activity happens often when you're dealing with transactions through Craigslist.

Do Not Give Out Your Telephone Number!

I never put my telephone number on any of my garage sale signs, or in any of the advertisements I place. If you list your telephone number, you'll have people calling you at all hours of the day and night.

Incoming calls about your sale will sometimes last for weeks after the sale is over. You really need to think seriously about whether or not you want to divulge your number to the general public, and exactly what the repercussions may be if you choose to do so. The only exception to this rule is if you give someone your telephone number because they are interested in buying an item from you after your garage sale ends.

Another reason not to display your number is that people don't value your time the same as you do. With the best of intentions, you give a customer your telephone number so they can call back regarding an item if they have any questions, or to arrange payment. The customer then decides to call you when you're in the middle of dinner after you've gone to bed for the night, or at any other extremely inconvenient time of day.

So, remember, when you do give out your telephone number, you must consider what could happen in a worst-case scenario. If you must advertise your telephone number, use only a cellular telephone number that you can control.

Do Not Sell Anything Illegal

You may read this and think it's the most ridiculous thing I could say. You might also say, "Of course, who would be dumb enough to sell illegal items?" It's not as stupid a statement as you might think. I've been to many garage sales where honest people have unknowingly sold illegal items. Besides the obvious illegality of selling drugs, drug paraphernalia, and fireworks, I need to clue you in on some very popular legal items that might be misconstrued as illegal under the right circumstances.

Firearms and ammunition comprise a significant percentage of goods sold at garage sales. However, if not sold properly, the sale can constitute an illegal act. People don't usually set out to sell entire arsenals of illegal firearms, but if they sell their firearms and ammunition improperly, they could end up serving jail time. If you want to sell firearms or ammunition, you will need to let a licensed gun store clear them for you first. Licensed gun stores will make all the proper background checks to ensure that people who are not allowed to purchase these items will not wind up getting them. Better yet, by going through licensed gun stores, you can almost assure yourself that you won't get into any legal trouble selling firearms. This does not count for black powder weapons. In some states, laws differ on selling weapons and ammunition at garage sales.

The worst-case scenario would be for you to sell a firearm improperly at your event, and then that firearm is used in the act of committing a crime. If this did happen, the authorities would come directly back to you, and you would be entangled in a web of legal problems.

> **Million $ Tip**
>
> Before donating your items, check every nook and cranny to make sure you aren't leaving any valuables behind. This includes dresser drawers, couch cushions, coat and bag pockets, and even hidden linings – you never know what valuable items might have been tucked away and forgotten about!

Fireworks are another item with tricky legal issues

regarding garage sales. Time and time again, I have seen people selling fireworks that are not legally allowed in their city or county. The worst-case scenario associated with selling fireworks is for someone to become injured or have an accident with the fireworks you sold them. Profits from fireworks, whether illegal or not, are never worth the risk if the product could potentially cause someone bodily harm. If a person gets hurt after they buy something from you, the most likely outcome will be that they will come back and aggressively sue you. We live in a very litigious society, if you haven't noticed already, and people are always looking for an easy way to make quick money from lawsuits. Be very mindful to ensure that anything you sell cannot harm anyone in any way.

Recalled items must never be sold at any garage sale. If you have something that has been recalled and you know it has been recalled, please don't ever try and sell it. The best thing you can do with any recalled item is throw it away or send it back to the manufacturer if there is a re-call notice. Obviously, you don't want to sell an item such as baby furniture or children's toys that pose a potential health risk to anyone's family. So please, if you know something could be harmful, especially if it has been officially recalled, don't sell that item. To see if your item is on a recall list, go to www.recalls.gov.

What Do You Do if You Can't Sell All of Your Items?

Here are some other possible options for disposing of things you couldn't sell at your garage sale. Earlier in this chapter, I described using a private trash-hauling company to come to your house and remove any remaining items. I also talked about taking your items to consignment and secondhand stores to see if they can resell any of your unsold items, giving you a portion of the proceeds. You can also donate these items to a 501c3 charity. The financial benefit of donating your unsold items to a charitable organization comes in the form of a potential tax write-off. Of course, please consult with your personal tax professional to get an exact idea of what you can or cannot deduct from any charitable donation. By donating items to charity, not only will you be helping others in need, but you will also be helping yourself as well.

Now You Can Have the World's Greatest Garage Sale

I have to say that buying items and selling items at estate auctions, garage sales and everything in between is a highly enjoyable activity to engage in, not to mention a highly profitable endeavor! Personally, I've had so much fun holding garage sales that I have hosted nearly 50 of them in my life, and I don't plan on stopping any time soon. I absolutely know you're going to have a tremendous time holding your own garage sales as well.

By actively participating in estate auctions, buying, and selling items online, and using other means to buy and sell collectibles as outlined in this chapter—in addition to holding garage sales—you'll soon be making yourself some serious money.

My Last Million $ Tip for the Garage Sale Millionaire

The information I've presented in this chapter has helped me buy and sell millions of dollars' worth of collectibles over the course of 50+ years—not only as a fine art and collectible gallery owner, but also as a Garage Sale Millionaire. If you adhere to the principles detailed in this chapter, you too can become a Garage Sale Millionaire.

Fortunately, all the profitable fun doesn't stop where this book ends. Please visit my website at **www.thegaragesalemillionaire.com** or on social media for more insider tips and need-to-know money-making information so I can continue to guide you in your quest to become the best Garage Sale Millionaire you can be! Also, if you have any questions about the book, the buying and selling process, or if you want to share your accomplishments with me, I'd love to hear from you at **thegaragesalemilionaire@gmail.com.** Maybe I could highlight your successes in the next edition of *The Garage Sale Millionaire!*

I hear remarkable success stories all the time from other Garage Sale Millionaires. You now have the essential tools to successfully navigate your own course to becoming a Garage Sale Millionaire too! Those hidden gems and buried treasures are always out there just waiting for you to discover them. Get out

Conclusion

I've had a lot of friends tell me I should teach others how I made my money, both growing up and again in saving my business. This book is meant to be a resource for other people to learn from. I truly believe that, if you follow the steps in this book, chapter by chapter, you should be able to go to any garage sale, estate sale, storage unit auction, or secondhand store, and feel comfortable looking at any of the items they have for sale, knowing that you are able to convert those items into cold hard cash.

Please, after you've read all of the chapters when you feel like it's time for you to go out on your own and start your new venture of becoming a Garage Sale Millionaire, don't get caught up in the excitement of an auction or a sale. Always do your research. Have fun. And good luck on your new journey to becoming a Garage Sale Millionaire.

Happy Hunting!

— Aaron LaPedis

About the Author

Long considered one of the world's great collectors and treasure hunters, Aaron LaPedis is a successful TV personality, former fine art and memorabilia gallery owner, expert for the FBI, and award-winning author of *The Garage Sale Millionaire.*

In this book, Aaron reveals many of the highly guarded secrets of successful and profitable treasure hunters. He has been interviewed on radio, and TV, and has been featured in numerous magazines and newspapers for his expertise on art and collectibles.

Aaron was the host of the highly rated PBS show in Denver, Colorado, called *Collect This!* In its last four years, it was one of the top PBS shows in Colorado.

Earlier versions of *Collect This!*, entitled *Collectibles with Aaron* and *The Collectibles Show,* first began airing in May of 2001 on PBS. Aaron successfully taped more than fifty half-hour segments focusing on the diverse world of collectors and collecting. A few of the topics covered were coins, wine, art, animation, and sports. His expertise in these subjects has made him an extremely popular and highly sought-after public speaker. Aaron's thoroughly personable and informative style entertains while teaching his audience how they can become better collectors and treasure hunters.

Aaron's expert credentials do not end with hosting his own TV show. The Discovery Channel featured him in their special, "What's America Worth", while *Entrepreneur* magazine published an article about his success as a master collector and successful entrepreneur. Aaron has also guest-hosted a collectibles show on Dish Network, written articles for Denver Magazine and the Denver Business Journal, and was a regular columnist for The Denver Post.

He has also hosted a weekly four-minute segment on the local Denver ABC affiliate, KMGH, called *The Collectibles Guy.*

Aaron is married to Sandee, and they have a son named Logan. Together, they opened Fascination St. Fine Art in Denver, Colorado in 1992. The gallery features original paintings, sculptures, and limited-edition artwork by the finest regional, national, and international artists. The fresh and new ideas of Fascination St. Fine Art were inspired by the travels of Aaron and Sandee.

In June of 2023, Aaron decided to sell the gallery and retire. Although he no longer owns the gallery, he is still readily involved in the art world and has an eBay store called The Garage Sale Millionaire, where he sells items of all kinds, like fine art, sports memorabilia, famous autographs, Disneyana, electronics, books, and more!

Despite being retired, Aaron will never cease his treasure hunting and is always on the lookout for a great deal. He has made himself into a truly successful *Garage Sale Millionaire,* and after reading this book, he hopes you will too.